W9-ANM-624

SOUTH AMERICA

WITH MEXICO AND CENTRAL AMERICA

By

J. B. TREND

Professor of Spanish in the University of Cambridge; Member of the Hispanic Society of America

OXFORD UNIVERSITY PRESS
LONDON · NEW YORK · TORONTO

OXFORD UNIVERSITY PRESS
AMEN HOUSE, E.C.4
London Edinburgh Glasgow New York
Toronto Melbourne Capetown Bombay
Calcutta Madras
HUMPHREY MILFORD
PUBLISHER TO THE UNIVERSITY

First published October 1941
Second Impression January 1942

PRINTED IN GREAT BRITAIN

To

ALFONSO REYES

IN

ADMIRATION AND FRIENDSHIP

CONTENTS

ILLUSTRATIONS

MAPS

ZAPOTEC INDIANS (MEXICO)

FROM THE SIERRAS
(*Paul Popper*)

IN OAXACA MARKET
(*Paul Popper*)

CHAPTER I

SPANISH AND PORTUGUESE AMERICANS

THE Spanish and Portuguese Americas are the nineteen independent republics south of the United States. If you include Haiti, which speaks French, there are twenty countries altogether. Their names are: Mexico; the island of Cuba; the island shared by Haiti and Santo Domingo; the six central American States of Guatemala, Honduras, Salvador, Nicaragua, Costa Rica and Panama; and the ten large countries of South America: Colombia, Venezuela, Ecuador, Peru, Brazil, Bolivia, Paraguay, Uruguay, Argentina and Chile.

For most people in the British Isles these countries are likely to remain countries of the mind, of the imagination; and the imagination does not always go very far. The first thought is apt to be of pathless tropical forests full of vampire bats and poisonous snakes; or a mountain range thousands of miles long, studded with volcanoes, or boundless grassy plains inhabited by wild cattle and horses, or immense rivers and swamps infested by alligators. If we look in shops and ask more questions, Spanish and Portuguese America may mean pineapples and bananas, dahlias and orchids, frozen carcases and tins of bully beef. To stockbrokers, it means mines, rails and oil; to dancers, it means the tango and the rumba, recorded by an *orquesta típica*; to philatelists, an extraordinary variety of postage-stamps.

One thing these Americas seldom mean to us, and that is people—over 110 millions of them: not Indians lurking in tropical forests and shooting explorers with poisoned arrows, or cowboys who live perpetually on horseback lassoing broncos, or rumba-dancers in barracas, or revolutionaries firing pistols at presidents; bu mainly people like ourselves, who have a job and no too much money and are very ready to be friendly i only we can talk each other's language.

Let us beware of statistics. Most writers on Americ overwhelm you with statistics, because they have bee overwhelmed by them themselves. To read that Argen tine beef exports amount to 515,208 metric tons a yea gives most of us less understanding of Argentina than t know how one cattle-farmer lives. "Relations" (a Uru guayan once said to me) "are not established betwee governments, but between individuals." My own earlie acquaintances included a Chilean doctor, a Bra zilian musician, an Ecuadorean sailor, a Mexican civ servant, two undergraduates from Panama, a Peruvia writer, and a Uruguayan classical scholar; and an haphazard collection of Spanish or Portuguese Ameri cans, met by accident, would probably consist of peopl whose jobs and lives and views are never mentioned i our Press, but who, with all their differences from ou selves, are only part of another busy, civilized society.

These American peoples may be different from us, bu in many ways they are even more different from on another. It is not only that they feel themselves to b Argentines or Brazilians or Colombians or Mexicans– citizens of independent and widely contrasting State as well as inhabitants of the Western Hemisphere They may be pure Spanish or Portuguese, half-India or half Irish or half Italian, pure Indian or full-bloode negro. The countries in which they live also show th greatest differences in appearance and climate. I Mexico the geography is comparatively simple. Ther is a backbone of mountains which are the tail of th Rockies. Round the coast is a low-lying tropical bel damp on the Atlantic side, generally desert on th Pacific. Then comes a middle semi-tropical zone fro about 2500 to 6000 ft. over the sea. Next comes th high Mexican plateau, mostly above 6000 ft., leading up to the Sierras and the volcanoes. The skeleton of South America is more complicated. There are first the Atlantic plateaux of the Guianas and Brazil, once joined to Africa. On the Pacific side is the Andean mountain system, a great wall running the whole length of the continent from north to south: to the north it divides into several smaller chains running east along the coast of the Caribbean Sea. The rest of the continent is low-lying: to the north the valleys of the Orinoco and the Amazon, with thousands of streams and impenetrable virgin forests, and to the south, on both sides of the River Plate, the great plain of the Pampa. Mexico and South America are joined by the narrow tropical isthmus of the six central States, less than 50 miles wide at the Panama Canal.

There is not enough physical unity to induce, by itself, a spirit of collaboration or "good-neighbourliness" between the peoples of all this territory. The sheer distances are difficult to grasp. Nicaragua is larger than England; Brazil is larger than the United States and half as large again as India. From Mexican ports to the tip of Chile is some 4000 miles by the Pacific route, and considerably more by the Atlantic. (Liverpool to New York is only three-quarters as far.) Communications are often extremely difficult. Many of the countries are hemmed in by high mountains or low-lying plains, which, with jungles and swamps, are a serious obstacle to the construction of roads and railways. The best routes about the continent are by sea and air; but few of these countries have had the money to build large shipping fleets for themselves, and air-travel is a new thing. The growth of air-lines has, however, profoundly modified the relations between them, and has already brought them to be better neighbours. Since 1937 all their capitals have been connected with the United States and with each other, so that the remotest can be reached from any other in about three days. A great continental motoring road, the Panamerican Highway, is under construction, from Boston to Buenos Aires. At present it is interrupted in the Panama Canal zone, and at various points in South America; the long stretch from Buenos Aires to the Andes was opened at the beginning of this year.

It must not be imagined that all these countries are everywhere tropical. Climate, in most regions of the continent, is more a matter of altitude than of latitude. A few hours' drive will take you from a steaming tropical afternoon at Veracruz into a cold sunset on the road to Mexico City. Hot jungles in Brazil lie due east of the high temperate zones of Peru and Ecuador; and most of Bolivia is over 10,000 ft. above sea-level and swept by bitterly cold winds. Farther south, Uruguay lies entirely within temperate latitudes, and so does a great part of Argentina. Chile stretches from a baked tropical desert, through a belt of Mediterranean type, into wet, cold forests, and is horizontally varied all the way down by the levels of the Andes. Most of these countries have a coast; some have coasts on both oceans; Bolivia and Paraguay are entirely land-bound, though the latter has river-communication with the Atlantic. These facts of geography and climate and their effects decide to a very large extent where the inhabitants of Latin America can live.

Compared with Europe or North America, the land is thinly populated. From 5 inhabitants to the square mile in Bolivia the distribution rises to 11·3 in Argentina and 27 in Uruguay; and in Central America (where the figures are less reliable) it is said to reach 95 in Cuba and 126 in Salvador. The returns for England and Wales are 703 per square mile, and for the Netherlands 640. Brazil has a population of 43 millions—nearly as high as that of Great Britain—but its area is slightly larger than the United States, which has 131 millions.

AN INDIAN OF PARA
(Paul Popper)

NEGRO QUARRYMAN
(Paul Popper)

BRAZILIAN TYPES

Within the several countries the density varies greatly, concentrating along the coasts or in valleys below the mountain tops or highlands above swamp and uncleared jungle.[1]

The population includes most of the races of the world. The original inhabitants seem to have been of Asiatic stock, and their remote ancestors came from Siberia across Bering Strait. Then for 400 years of colonial empire immigrants came almost entirely from Spain and Portugal; subjects of other countries were not legally admitted, and in practice it was difficult for them to get in. There was, however, one other important source of immigration: negro slaves. Something like 12 million, it is said, were shipped to Brazil from Africa; and to the West Indies they were brought in great and increasing numbers, chiefly on the advice of Padre de las Casas, the Apostle of the Indies, who saw how quickly the Indian natives died from the work in mines and plantations which the Spaniards set them to do.

After the Spanish and Portuguese possessions gained their independence early in the nineteenth century, immigrants reached South America from every country in Europe; more especially from the middle of the century (after the disturbances and persecutions of 1848) down to the slump of 1931, when most countries put a check on immigration and established a quota. Besides Europeans, a few Chinese have settled on the Pacific coast, mostly as small shopkeepers; Japanese have arrived in increasing numbers in Brazil, to work on carefully organized Japanese farms; and some Syrians have come to Mexico: you can see their tombstones in Mérida (Yucatán), with inscriptions in Arabic.

[1] The populations of the larger Latin American countries, for 1941, were estimated as follows: Brazil, 43 millions; Mexico, 19; Argentina, 13; Colombia, 9; Peru, 7; Chile, 5; Cuba, 4·4; Venezuela, 3·4; Bolivia, 3·3; Ecuador, 3; Guatemala, 3; Uruguay, 2·8; Paraguay, 1.

These later immigrants are not everywhere nor completely assimilated. Many non-Spanish Europeans have
become to all intents and purposes Chileans and Argentines; but there are considerable colonies, especially
British and German, which resist absorption. Italians
are readier to become American, but they also provide
a steady stream of "swallow-workers" who stay in the
country only for a year or so.

Negroes are numerous only in Brazil and about the
coasts of Colombia, Venezuela, and Ecuador; and they
are now beginning to be assimilated, except at Bahia
(Brazil), which was the largest slave-market until slavery was abolished in 1888. There they keep their racial
purity and their astonishing dances.

Brazil differs from all the other republics not only in
speaking Portuguese, but also in its large admixture of
negro blood. Over 50 per cent. of the population is,
indeed, white; but the rest is extensively mixed with
the black race, which is far commoner than the brown.[1]
Portugal never caught the colour-prejudice of modern
European imperialism, but retained the medieval toler-
ance; and it has bequeathed to Brazil its capacity for
racial assimilation. To Brazilians, the Aryan heresy of
the Nazis would be unintelligible. Some of them believe
in the ideal of a "cosmic" race which shall be as mixed
as possible. They admit no colour-bar, and the standard of living of the negroes is much the same as that
of the rest of the people. Such distinction as they have
ever recognized has been not racial, but social: in the
seventeenth and eighteenth centuries a man with negro
blood became "white", and his relations counted as
whites, if he was elected to an exclusive religious
brotherhood.

[1] The racial composition in 1922 was given by a Brazilian
source as follows: White, 51 per cent.; White and Black, 22;
Black, 14; White and Indian, 11; Indian, 2. The percentage of
zambos (Black and Indian) is not available.

In the Spanish American countries it is the Indian admixture, not the negro, which determines the race. A man born of European ancestry is called a *criollo*; a man of mixed Spanish and Indian blood is known as *mestizo*. But visitors must be very careful in the use of these terms. Many Spanish Americans would think it snobbish, and therefore bad manners, to classify people in this way. It is only in Argentina and Uruguay, the two *criollo* countries, that people pride themselves on being *criollos*. (In Argentina the word is often used as equivalent to "national".) Elsewhere it may, as in old Brazil, imply a social distinction: in Bolivia it is said that an Indian turns into a *mestizo* by a change of clothes, and a *mestizo* becomes a *criollo* by acquiring land. But there is no purely racial snobbery between *criollos* and *mestizos*: many Spanish Americans, like many North Americans, are proud of a dash of Indian blood. The general attitude, outside Argentina and Uruguay, is only a little less liberal than in Brazil. It might perhaps be said that, whereas the Brazilian ideal could be called "cosmic" in its wider implications, the Spanish American ideal is specifically American. The consciousness of mixed blood and pride in it—pride in not being European, but American—is producing a distinctive outlook on life. It is an outlook unreservedly generous in its acceptance of all types and races o men, but intensely opposed to interference in America affairs and institutions, both from foreigners and from the Church. The basis of political life is not *Blut un Boden*—"Blood and Soil"—but, more than anywher else, a community of traditions and ideals. The wor *hispanidad*, for instance, properly means a "Spanish ness" of culture, language, and outlook, and does no exclude any *mestizo* who shares in these things. Foreig propagandists from Europe have recently tried to giv a racial twist to the conception of *hispanidad;* but such meaning is quite alien to Spanish America.

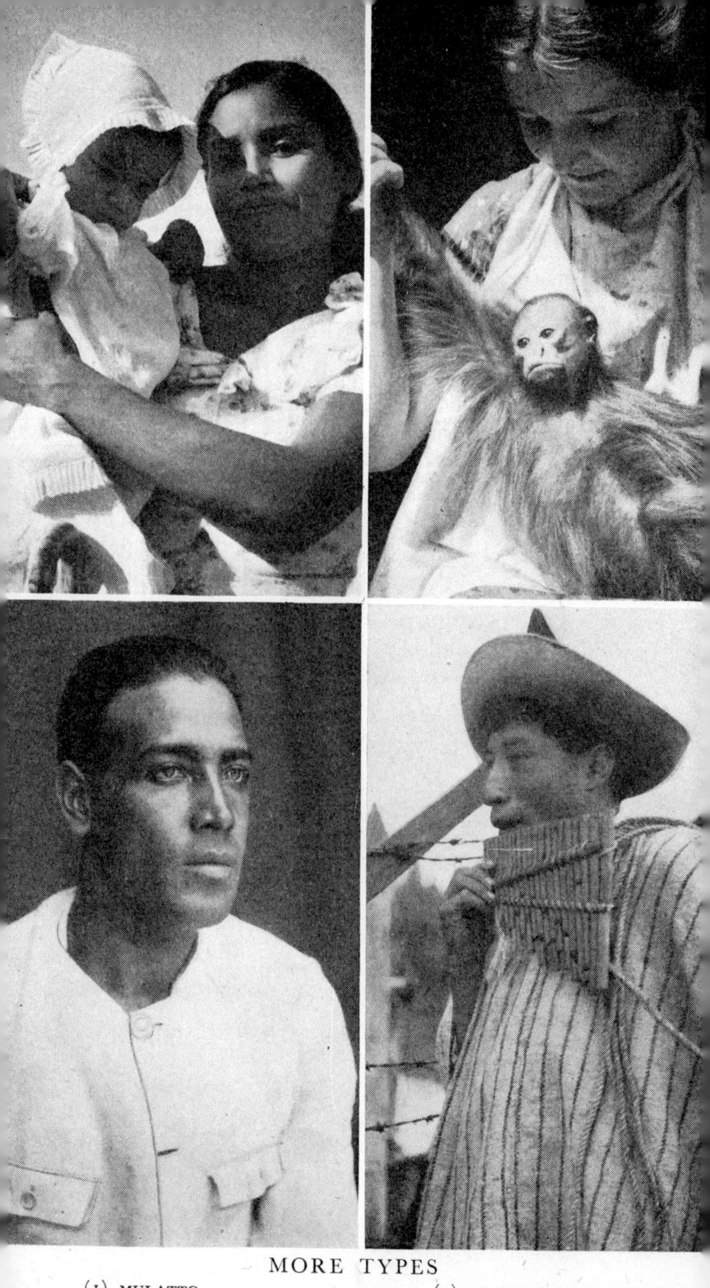

MORE TYPES

(1) MULATTO
(*Paul Popper*)

(2) BRAZILIAN PORTUGUESE
(*Paul Popper*)

(3) MESTIZO (VENEZUELA)
(*Fox Photos*)

(4) INDIAN PIPER (ECUADOR)
(*Mondiale, Ltd.*)

The variety of races and the mixtures which are resulting will make Spanish and Portuguese America, far more than the United States, the great racial experiment of the future. The proportions of the mixture, however, vary from one country to another; and where there are large numbers of Indians who, for one reason or another, have not been mixed with the European stock, special and urgent problems arise. Colombia, Venezuela, Paraguay, and Mexico, for instance, are mainly *mestizo* countries, but also contain large Indian populations; while Ecuador, Bolivia, Peru, and Guatemala are predominantly Indian.

The name of Indian covers a great many different types, cultures, and languages. Before the Spaniards came, the Aztecs in Mexico and the Incas in Peru had built up remarkable civilizations and created great works of art; whereas the Indians of Colombia, Venezuela, and Brazil had neither the culture nor the courage to resist the invaders, and have either died out or melted into other races, or retreated into the savage life of the jungle. In Chile, the Araucanians and Mapuches were fine fighting men, who first put up a fierce struggle against the Spaniards and then contributed their qualities to the well-compounded stock of the modern Chilean working people. In Cuba, the gentle friendly Indians whom Columbus found, dancing their native dances and smoking tobacco, were soon exterminated by the hard work which the Spanish conquerors imposed. Within a single country, such as Mexico, Indians may be villagers or nomads, and may speak any one of fifty-odd languages.

So far as any generalizations can hold good in such variety, it seems that the Indians are ill-adapted to tropical climates; but in temperate zones or in the mountains they still hold their own as a component of the population, and have seldom been displaced from their original homes. In Mexico, for instance, the white man and the *mestizo* have settled in towns or have populated those parts of the countryside which before the conquest were uninhabited or traversed only by nomad groups. The Indian population, however, is threatened in many countries by an infant mortality which can rise to 80 per cent. even among the vigorous Mayas of Yucatán, and by physical degeneration due to indulgence in coca, which is ruining the natives of Bolivia and Peru.

Even if the Indians can keep up their numbers, that does not mean that they are playing a full part as citizens of America. In the Andean republics, in spite of much intermarriage with the white men, great numbers of pure Indians are left insulated, as a nation within a nation; and a baffling problem is presented in Peru by those Indians who steadily refuse to do any kind of work. The Mexican Indians, though they are clever at village handicrafts, have not often been found capable of industrial labour; and it is only within the ast few years that any effort has been made to teach Indians to read and write. Many cannot speak Spanish. In Paraguay, the local Indian lingua franca, *Guaraní*, is a second national language, spoken by the less educated people. Newspapers print a column in Guaraní, and business men often speak it to their secretaries.

Among the many Indian tongues of Spanish America [1] some have a literature which is still preserved. A certain amount has been written in Quéchua, the language of the descendants of the Incas: and more in the Mexican languages Náhuatl (Aztec), Maya, and Tarascan. The following verse from a sixteenth-century

[1] In Mexico the chief languages are: Náhuatl (Aztec), spoken o-day by about 680,000 persons; Maya, 235,000; Otomí and apotec, 220,000; Mixtec, 170,000; Totonac, 60,000; Tarascan, 5,000. In South America the mountain languages include uéchua (pronounced "Ketch-wa"), in Ecuador, Peru, and olivia; Aymará, in Peru and Bolivia; Chibcha, in the Colombian ndes; Araucanian, in Chile. Among the lowland languages are rawak, Carib, and Tupi-Guaraní.

Aztec poem is preserved in one of the old Spanish grammars of the language:

> Quemmach huel tehuantin, in otiquittaque in ipololoca in Mexicayotl!
>
> (Alas that to us, it was given to see the destruction of our Mexican Empire!)

Lope de Vega, in a Spanish play on the conquest of Chile, wrote a song with a nonsense-refrain intended to suggest the Araucanian language:

> Piraguamonte, piragua,
> piragua, jevizarizagua.[1]

There has been plenty of cruelty and exploitation in the treatment of the Indians, from the time of the Conquest down to the Putumayo rubber atrocities thirty years ago; and many of the less virile peoples have been wiped out. Conditions have improved since then but it is clear that the Indians cannot be made healthy or useful partners in American civilization either by the mild form of slavery known as peonage or by simply leaving them alone. A race which once ruled a busy empire, suddenly deprived of all intelligent share in social life, is easily driven to coca or to mere passivity. Recently, many of the republics have been making conscious efforts to protect the Indians and to raise their standard of living, both material and intellectual. Mexico, in the last twenty years, has done excellent work with its lay missions and with schools to instruct Indians, using their own languages, in farming and hygiene, as well as reading and writing. There are also schools for the training of native teachers. A meeting with a Mexican Indian *maestro rural*, or country schoolmaster, is a very interesting experience. In Guatemala, too, attempts have been made to teach the Indians to read in one of their languages (Cakchiquel), but the work is not encouraged by the authorities.

[1] *Oxford Book of Spanish Verse* (1940), No. 295.

In Colombia and Venezuela, where some groups of ndians live in complete savagery, certain tribes have een put under the care of Church missions. Peru has a *atronato*, a committee in charge of Indian welfare, but t has not so far touched the uncivilized Indians of the nterior. In Chile special laws for the Indians have been n force since 1930, and missions are at work in Arau-anian territory and among the tribes near the Straits f Magellan.

The most striking achievements in the protection of ndians have been carried out in Brazil, by General andido Rondon. For forty years General Rondon ombined exploring and engineering with continuous are for the native tribes in whose territory he worked. he Government appreciated his efforts, and he was iven wide powers to deal with the Indian problem. Commissão Rondon was formed, and has done much teach the Indians cattle-breeding and crop-growing, hile preserving their territories and hunting- and fish-g-grounds, so as to leave them free to follow their old omadic habits if they choose. The Indians of Brazil re, however, comparatively few, and are likely to main a small minority in the population.

If such efforts as these can increase the physical and cial vitality of the Indians, it is possible that Spanish merica (north of Argentina and Uruguay, and ex-uding Brazil) may eventually be a continent in which dian characteristics will gain great importance. This as been foreseen by many American thinkers and poli-cians. Two courses of action have suggested them-lves. Until lately, the ideal of administrators was the olicy of incorporation—bringing the Indians in—so at they might take a share in modern civilization. he results have not come up to expectations. Though e white and brown races have been mixing more and ore, the pure Indians seem to preserve their ethnic tonomy, and are not ready to throw themselves into the life of modern America. Another current of opinion is that it is a mistake to seek to incorporate Indians in a civilization which is, to them, exotic. They have never succeeded in digesting Spanish culture in the past, and they probably never will. Spain conquered the territory, but was never able to conquer the soul of the Indians. A more modern view, therefore, is "that it is necessary to build on the basis of what the Indian is developing his peculiar faculties and his agricultura and political organization in such a way that he wil become an active helper in the creation of a new national culture, which may express the life of both Indian and *mestizo* alike".[1]

So as Spanish America evolves out of its colonial pas and becomes more American, there is a chance that the original inhabitants may find their way back into the life of the continent, and may in their turn modify it future.

The achievement of the Spanish and Portuguese Americas during their century of independence is one o the great facts of modern history. Yet their prospects their possibilities for the future, are even more attrac tive. Their civilization is still a brilliant fringe, carried forward inch by inch on the edge of jungles or deserts and up the face of high mountains. Whether in towns or in cultivated lands, or in the wired cattle-ranches c the Pampa, it has only been won by effort. In som places the effort has failed, and a town is swallowed u by the encroaching jungle or returns to the condition c an Indian settlement. Almost everywhere, more coun try remains to be opened up and made productive.

The life of the Spanish and Portuguese Americas mainly country life; yet only modern inventions ca fight back the natural forces of such an intractabl continent, and only modern social ideas can overcom the human inertia which such difficulties have som

[1] *The Republics of South America* (Oxford, 1937).

times induced. Both the inventions and the ideas have come lately into the hands of the Latin American peoples, and their next hundred years may see even greater advances than their last. They have not yet done all that they mean to do. That is perhaps why they are among the few peoples in the world whose belief in progress has not been shaken, and whose ideals —however hopeless they might appear in Europe—are to them plans which can be put into practice.

CHAPTER II

DISCOVERY, COLONIZATION, AND INDEPENDENCE

THE story of the discovery and colonization of America by the Spaniards and Portuguese has been told too often, and too well, for it to be told again here. To speak patronizingly of it, or "de-bunk" it, is impossible. The motives of the conquistadores may be reduced to their lowest terms, but their ideals compare favourably with those of other empire-builders; while there were jurists in Spain and administrators in the colonies with a sense of trusteeship in Empire which seems strangely modern. There was also a medieval side to the discovery. It was as if the dreams of the poets had been realized; and while to the conquistadores the dream was as real as the gold, to philosophers it seemed that the Golden Age had been discovered in another sense: in the simple lives of the Indians.

Until a few years ago, most writers on the expansion of Spain—and, above all, English writers—had been inclined to take too romantic a view; and romanticism is not poetry, any more than it is history or economics. It was not that they concentrated too much on biography—it was that most of them concentrated in the wrong way.[1] We must not regard the Spanish expeditions as Everest expeditions: a test of endurance with a few scientific observations, a sport raised to the power of mysticism. Most of the English writers on Spanish exploration and colonization have given us too much romantic geography and not enough of the human

[1] See, however, F. A. Kirkpatrick, *The Spanish Conquistadores*, 1934—a book which has earned the distinction of translation into Spanish.

ture—and poetry—of trading and economics. The
dours and endurances of the Spanish explorers have
come a commonplace, because they have been given
romantic or mystical interpretation; but since his-
rical research on the Spanish colonial period has been
riously conducted on modern lines it has completely
anged the perspective in which the events can be
ewed. It has been able to do this because, for the
st time, it can apply a thorough knowledge of the
cial, economic, and political institutions concerned.

Columbus and the Nightingale

Yet it should never be forgotten that there was a side
the discoveries which seemed to many people living
the time like a dream come true: the medieval dream
the Earthly Paradise. The dream-world of these
en—"dream-captains of dream-ships", a modern
anish poet has called them—is clearly revealed in the
itings of those who went there and took part in this
eatest of all adventures. A tropical island like Santo
omingo, where Columbus landed on December 6th,
92, seemed like the biblical island of Ophir. He
uld only describe what he saw in the simplest words,
e words that came into his mind first; yet a careful
ading of his letter gives the impression that he is un-
nsciously repeating something which he has heard
fore; that there is, in fact, some literary influence at
e back of it. Columbus—like the old Spanish poet
nzalo de Berceo, two generations before Dante—is
scribing the garden of the Earthly Paradise in the
nguage (as he said) of a man speaking to his neigh-
ur, or like Dante himself in the dense forest of the
rgatorio. Columbus had probably never read a line
Berceo, or of Dante either; but the idea of the
rthly Paradise so haunted him on his voyages that
almost came to believe that he had discovered it.

> The trees were so tall that they seemed to touc the sky; . . . and never lost their leaves so far a I could understand it; for I saw them as green an fresh in November as they are in Spain in Ma and some were in flower and some with fruit . . and the nightingale was singing, and other birds i thousands of kinds wherever I went.

Columbus is like a traveller in a fabulous regic of eternal spring. His excitement can be felt, as h struggles to describe what he saw in such simple word as he had. His sincerity cannot be doubted; yet the on positive fact that he mentions is the song of the nigh ingale, and the nightingale has never been known i America. Columbus's nightingale is a literary remini cence, from those descriptions of the fabled gardens the Earthly Paradise; and a bird which sang the could hardly have been called anything else.[1] Indee the Earthly Paradise itself was not far off; and Cal fornia was named from an island "on the right har of the Indies, very near the Earthly Paradise", me tioned in a chivalrous romance, *Las Sergas* ("exploits or "tapestries") *de Esplandián*, which was one of tl books in the library of Don Quixote.

The discoveries of Columbus gave the Spaniards footing in Cuba and Santo Domingo; and from the they were able to send out expeditions to explore tl American continent. This they did so rapidly, that i a comparatively short time they could claim to ad minister territories extending from about Lat. 4 South, in Chile and Paraguay, to points touching La 41° or 42° North, and now included in the Unite States.[2]

[1] Leonardo Olschki, *Storia letteraria delle scoperte geografic* (Florence, 1937).

[2] The following account is based on the most recent Americ researches, and on the work of Fernando de los Ríos in *Concerni Latin American Culture* (New York: Columbia University Pre 1940), and the *Proceedings of the Sixth International Congress Philosophy*, 1925.

The chief stages in the growth of the Spanish ›minions were:

1513. Discovery of the Pacific Ocean by Núñez de Balboa.
1519. Conquest of Mexico by Cortés.
1531–35. Conquest of Peru by Pizarro.
1533. Discovery of Lower California by Hurtado de Mendoza. (Meanwhile De Soto and Pineda had discovered the Mississippi.)
1534–38. Discovery of the River Plate.
1540. Vásquez de Coronado extends Spanish dominion over a vast region now part of the United States.
1540–41. Extension to Chile.

ı North America the extent of Spanish progress can e deduced to a certain extent from place-names: there a town called Las Vegas a little north of Lat. 36°, nd a San Jacinto north of 41°. In the State of Oregon :he southern boundary of which runs on the 42nd arallel) there are also places with Spanish names; but is not known whether these were Spanish colonial ettlements or not—*e.g.*, Bonanza, Estacada. In Colorado, north-west of Denver, there is a Fort Vasques names after Vásquez de Coronado); and this is probbly the most advanced point which the Spaniards eached.

It will be seen that something like 60 or 70 years ere enough to implant Spanish rule on the American ontinent from Chile and Argentina up to Mexico, nd eventually as far as Colorado and Florida. The nly exceptions were the Guianas and Brazil, and the nly important island lost was Jamaica, which became ritish in 1655. What did Spain do with this vast erritory?

The Spanish Administrators

It is sometimes carelessly assumed that Spanis colonial administration was inefficient. On the co trary, after the first shock of the discovery it was car fully planned by the home Government and carrie out in America by able men. From the beginnin the chief difficulties were the distance from Spai and the time that instructions from home took to reac colonial officials; and by the end of the eighteenth cen tury it was clear that the system was too rigid. Sligh modifications, however, were being introduced a through the colonial period. The Spanish system wa in complete contrast with the almost uncontrolle colonization, carried out by British settlers, acting i groups or as isolated individuals in North Americ The Spanish settlement was from the first an offici undertaking, conducted on the methodical principle of a government department.

Yet the action of Spain in America cannot be under stood without distinguishing between the views of th Spanish Government at home and the demands c colonial society in America. The Government was re presented in the colonies by administrators eager t apply the policy of trusteeship which was favoured i many quarters in Spain. They were met at every tur by the ambition and acquisitiveness of the colonists and the struggle between them was once again th struggle between two forces which have always bee active in the Peninsula, and elsewhere—the clash be tween ideals and interests. The discovery of Americ had accentuated the divergence between the two for there was always a difference between wha was said in royal decrees and what was done b officials and settlers on the spot, and students of th history of Spain have been inclined to judge Spanis colonial policy according to whether they stress th ıe or the other. It is necessary, of course, to consider ɔth. While Spanish statesmen had a theory of "natural w" (defining the relation of the conqueror to the ɒnquered), and were anxious to put their theories into ·actice, the forces on the spot in America were more terested in maintaining the social system as it was Europe. Profiting by the weakness and inexːrience of the Indians, they endeavoured to strengthen .eir own position. The Spaniards brought to America l their social prejudices as well as their social institu- ɔns, and these institutions—though the intention was purify them, and put them more in harmony ith the new principles of "natural law"—still .owed signs of their origin, in the old struggle be- veen ideals and interests. Their principles came into olent collision with the acquisitive impulses of Spanish dividuals, which were even stronger in America than .ey had been in Spain.

The statesman, however, had on his side the Church. is guiding principle was religious, and in his culture, ›o, the emphasis was laid on the duty of saving souls. he Church was the chief instrument with which Spain ied to shape the destinies of the new countries, and should be kept clearly in mind that the Spanish hurch acted under orders of the State, not of the Pope.

In sixteenth-century Spain, a man of education, ıergy, and resource—like so many of the young men the "Exemplary Novels" of Cervantes—had two ıreers open to him; or three if *Casa real*, service at ourt, is included. The two careers were military and vil. Don Quixote called them arms and letters— ːms including exploration in America as well as mili- ıry service in Flanders, and letters including the Law well as the Church; so that it was not such a change ›r one of the greatest Spanish colonial reformers, asco de Quiroga, to pass from the office of *Oidor* to ıat of Bishop. There was an *Oidor* (civil judge), we re-

member, on his way to embark for the Indies, w
stayed at the same inn as Don Quixote.

Sixteenth-century Spaniards, like the Elizabetha
were men of tireless energy. Both types, the man
letters no less than the man at arms, were combativ
they were eager to conquer, to succeed; and while t
man of military temperament wished to succeed
power, command, territory, wealth, the more letter
would rather plan for a practical Utopia or save so
for Christianity. The two sometimes existed togeth
in the same individual; and the fact that both ide
were occasionally found in the same person came to
of the greatest legal and political importance. We ha
to realize the close association between the two
order to understand the leaders of Spanish colonizatio

There is, of course, plenty of room for criticis
Cruelty, greed, fanaticism can be attributed to ma
of them; but what is beyond dispute is their firmness
adversity, and the blend of foresight and recklessn
with which they undertook the most daring enterpris
Left alone, or left in a responsible position, in surroun
ings that were strange to them, instead of being alarm
they felt attracted by the mystery; and they we
forward because they had a blind faith in their own wi
power and the importance of their mission.

The conquistadores were not the only men who fe
this; the feeling was shared by the missionaries, and eve
by the planters, as it was by the judges, the governo
and the Viceroy himself. Each knew that he was servi
a purpose—one predominant purpose—for which h
put forth every effort. He felt himself to be an instr
ment; though what he was an instrument of, he prob
ably could not have explained very clearly.

The Legal Position

That was left for the legists at home. They under-
od. The sixteenth century was the great period for
gal studies in Spain; and the men at the head of
eir profession—the men whom the Spanish kings
nsulted on matters concerning the Indies—were men
outstanding ability. One of the first and most prac-
al questions they had to settle was the legal relation
tween those who planned and organized the expedi-
ns, and the Crown. Expeditions were planned in
ree different ways:

(1) There were expeditions organized directly by
e State, and financially supported by it—*e.g.*, some
the voyages of Columbus, and those of Magellan
d Pedrarias de Avila.

(2) Expeditions were sometimes organized by the
ate in partnership with groups of individuals, and
pported jointly. These gave rise to the *capitulaciones*,
contracts of remuneration to the conquerors and in-
stors, offered as a reward for services rendered
d for the risk of the investment. This was the case
th most of the voyages of Columbus and several that
lowed.

(3) There were expeditions authorized by the
own, but controlled, both on the military and the
ancial sides, by private enterprise. In these cases,
e rights, privileges, and benefits reserved as a reward
each of the participants were fixed by the *capitula-
nes*. This type of expedition was the most usual.
was the case with the expedition of Cortés, and be-
me eventually the only kind of expedition which
s authorized.

The contractual origin of the *capitulación*, and the
ture of the contract, had a great influence on the

results of the expedition and the type of colonizat
it produced; and when the time came for the land
be distributed, it certainly encouraged the rapacity
those who had joined the expedition as "soldiers
fortune," merely to get rich quick.

There were, however, other legal questions, less i
mediately practical but more fundamentally importa
questions concerning the original owners of the lan
the Indians.

As soon as Ferdinand and Isabella heard that th
were numbers of people in their dominions who w
ignorant of everything Christian, they began to ins
on the duty of converting them to Christianity. Wh
any local commander discovered or conquered n
territory, the first thing he had to do was to procla
to the inhabitants that

> he had been sent to teach them good customs,
> dissuade them from such vices as the eating
> human flesh, and to instruct them in the h
> faith and preach it to them for their salvation.

That was the text of the *requerimiento*, the speech
be read to the Indians on reaching or occupying th
territory, or before undertaking military operatio
against them. The obligation was taken literally;
late as 1542 the Viceroy, Antonio de Mendoza, order
the *requerimiento* to be read (like the Riot Act) befo
firing on a crowd of rebellious Indians in Mexico. T
Act was read in Spanish, and entrusted to a friar w
was compelled to stand out of range, and presumab
therefore, out of earshot as well; but the requireme
of law and justice were held to have been fulfilled.
should have preferred to make sure that they unde
stood what was being said," a witness remarked
another occasion. "I afterwards asked Dr Pálaci
Rubios, the author of the *requerimiento*, whether t
reading sufficed to clear the consciences of t

BOLIVIA AND PERU

ON LAKE TITICACA (3 miles high).
(*Mondiale, Ltd.*)

LLAMAS IN THE ANDES
(*Fox Photos*)

Spaniards; he replied that it did, if carried out in the proper form."[1]

Yet some people in Spain, and particularly thos who would now be called international lawyers, begar to ask themselves where they stood. What was thei legal position? What legitimate title had they to remair in America? Palacios Rubios made a judicial summing-up of the question. "If", he said, "we make wa because they are infidels, then they can defend themselves; and their war will be just, but ours will be unjust." He came to the conclusion that the only titl Spain had was a spiritual title, given by the Pope.

That also was the argument of Francisco de Victoria one of the first to reach the conception of internationa law, in his lectures at Salamanca in 1539.[2] There wa undoubtedly a title, he held, and undoubtedly a mission. There were religious titles and lay titles: the former based on the right to preach and convert, the latte justified by humanitarian reasons. The presence c Spaniards in America was justified only in so far as th Spanish colonists bore these titles in mind. Victoria' position was not unlike the present conception of th mandate of the League of Nations.[3] It was also th position of Vasco de Quiroga, the judge who became bishop: "The Church orders us to win over faithfu brethren," he said. "On this understanding our prince hold the land and possess it; to interpret their possessio in any other way is blindness of heart."

This spiritual purpose was to be accomplished by th State. The State had obtained the *patronato* (guardianship or trusteeship) of the Indies; and in virtue of thi its power over the Church was almost unlimited. Ther was no appeal against its decisions. The Spanis

[1] J. H. Parry, *The Spanish Theory of Empire* (Cambridge, 1940
[2] J. B. Scott, *The Spanish Origin of International Law* (Oxford Carnegie Endowment for International Peace, 1934).
[3] Fernando de los Ríos, *op. cit.*, 56.

tate was openly secular and nationalist in its views.
Not all churchmen would accept this position, or
leal faithfully with the State, and in America some
f the orders connived at the most grasping and un-
rincipled of the adventurers. Yet a large minority in
he Spanish Church certainly did its duty. Franciscans,
Dominicans, and Jesuits crossed the wildest and most
langerous parts of Central and South America with no
ess courage than the conquistadores themselves. They
vere remarkable, too, for their human understanding
f the Indians, for their ready sympathy and linguistic
bility in securing the voluntary submission of hundreds
f scattered tribes to a new and difficult conception of
eligion and government.

The question of the legal position of the Spaniards in
America led to others. Should the Indians be considered
uman beings? Were they capable of living according
o Christian ideas? Las Casas was not the only man
vho defended the cause of the Indians, or claimed that
hey were human. Others did so, with less passion, per-
aps, but with greater equanimity and efficiency.
When Ferdinand summoned the Junta of Burgos in
512 to decide what attitude Spain should adopt to-
vards the Indians, the Assembly recognized their
iberty and their right to be treated in a humane
nanner, but compelled them to submit to firm juris-
liction. That was the basis of the Burgos law of 1512,
upplemented in 1515. It laid stress on education;
hurches were to be built in Indian villages, for the
eaching of religion as well as the celebration of mass.
The Spanish inhabitants were ordered not to commit
cts of violence against the Indians, but to treat them
vith humanity, and to choose the ablest as future
eachers. The law also laid down humane labour
egulations.

Encomienda and Misión

The two most characteristic institutions in the Spanish empire were the *Encomienda* and the *Misión*. From the beginning there had been pressure from the colonists, and those who supported them at home, in favour of slavery, or at any rate some form of forced labour, as the only means of ensuring the colonies' existence. The idea of Columbus had been frankly to establish a slave trade, as the Portuguese did in Brazil but that was not acceptable in Spain. The problem first came to a head when the Indians of Santo Domingo refused to work for the Spaniards at all, even for wage or even to till their own lands. The Spanish Government had either to find a way out, a formula permitting forced labour in fact if not in name, or to abandon the island entirely; and that might have meant that their empire would have extended no further. Instruction were sent that the Indians should be compelled to work on the land or in mines or on buildings, but always a free men. This, however, soon led to a distribution of men and land among the Spanish colonists, who thu became *encomenderos* of the Indians "commended" to their charge.

Yet, even so, the service of a number of Indians wa not often of much use without the land on which they worked. The colonist would come to watch his Indians at work in the maize-fields; and gradually, by a very natural process, he would come to regard the fields in which his Indians worked as his own property. Tha was an idea which the Indians were unable to understand. The natives in many parts of America were, in a sense, communists: they had little or no conception of private property in land. So long as they wer allowed to use it, it did not matter to them who claimed to be the owner of the property. But after th coming of the Spaniards, the Indians rapidly decreased in numbers; and many fields were left empty without any Indians to work in them or occupy them in their original communal form of possession. The result was that most of the land on which the *encomienda* Indians lived became the property of the Spaniards; and the system, though its object had been very different, came in the end to be a means of acquiring landed property.

In some parts of Spanish America—on the high Mexican plateau, for instance—the *encomiendas* openly took the form of grants of land, Indians and all included; and the deed of conveyance (for that was what the royal grant had practically become) was worded in a slightly different form: instead of being "the Cacique So-and-so, with his Indians", it became such and such a *pueblo*, or village, with its communally held fields and water, grasslands and woods. The *encomienda* thus came to give the Spaniards actual possession (understood to be temporary, of course) of the native agricultural communities and the lands they occupied; and this happened not only in the high valley of Mexico, but also in those agricultural districts (at that time densely populated) on the high plateaux of the Andes.

With land and labour thus distributed among the conquistadores and the officers of the Crown, the age of greatest abuses set in; while in Spain there began a struggle for ideals, which led to impassioned polemics from both sides. The men on the spot, who had to make the colony pay as well as making their own fortunes, were relentless with their logic of facts. They knew the Indians—knew just what they were worth, and it was not much. Las Casas and other members of religious orders had also been on the spot, and were unsparing in their criticism of the *encomienda* and its abuses. The Crown vacillated. Sometimes it spoke out for a more humane treatment of the Indians, and even declared that the *encomienda* could not be allowed to go on; sometimes it temporized, and seemed to think tha what had been done could not be undone. Presently even churchmen could be heard explaining that, afte all, there were various degrees of servitude, some mor tolerable and more justifiable than others, and tha slavery had been accepted by Aristotle. The promul gation of the Laws of Burgos was the first official repl to the establishment of the *encomienda*; but these law only led to more bitterness. It was at this time tha Las Casas appeared at his greatest; but the questio increased in complexity with each fresh discussion, an to some minds the benefit of the Indians seemed of les importance than the refutation of Aristotle's theory o slavery. Charles V declared the Indians to be citizen of Castille, and forbade their being made slaves (1526) but neither the moral authority of the king nor hi express command had any effect, and in the colonie no attention was paid either to Crown officials or priest or monks when they expressed opinions on the em ployment or condition of the Indians. The laws of 154 laid it down that personal service could not be de manded of an Indian, only tribute; and this left a loop hole by which the practice might in some sense b justified. The Indians could not pay in cash; so th Spaniards were authorized to collect their contributio in services. Conditions generally seem to have im proved after 1550. It is stated that the system wa never so harsh on the mainland as on the island o Santo Domingo, where it had first been introduced that it civilized the Indians and was culturally superio to the Mission. It gradually grew into the paternal tutelary relation of landowner and farm-labourer, an by the eighteenth century Spanish America came t have the normal structure of an agrarian society.

The *Misión*, though it, too, came to an end in th eighteenth century, was certainly a more interestin xperiment. It was no ordinary mission. It arose as a rotest against the rapacity of the conquistadores when hey became planters, and the exploitation of the ndians through the *encomienda*. The defenders of the ndians, seeing that in the prolonged controversy over he *encomienda* they were gaining very little for the ndian and not doing him much good, organized the rst missions as examples. They represented the ideal ocial order which the legal supporters of the Indians ad described in the course of their defence, a type of ociety capable of defending the Indians from every buse. Missions were established in all parts of the panish Empire, from the River Plate to Florida, New Aexico and California, from Mexico to Peru, and from Colombia to Paraguay and Argentina.

The original idea of a Mission—and the subject of he Spanish missions must be regarded without sentinentalism, and without anti-clericalism—owed somehing to More's *Utopia*, which itself had been sugested by the discovery of unspoiled peoples in America. Later missions were influenced by another deal republic, Campanella's *City of the Sun* (1623). Vasco de Quiroga knew the *Utopia* very well. He may ven have had a copy (the Louvain edition of 1516) vith him in Mexico, and frequently refers to it in his etters home on the condition of the Indians in Mihoacán.[1]

What were dreams to More and Campanella, became ctions with the Spanish missionaries—actions which hey did not consider so much as social experiments, out things done because they were a practical solution of the difficulty. Yet as social experiments they are very nteresting. Citizenship was based on labour for the ommunity; but the supreme magistrate was not the hilosopher (as in Plato) but the priest (as in Campa-

[1] Silvio A. Zavala, *La "Utopia" de Tomás Moro en la Nueva España* (Mexico, 1937).

nella). Public lands were worked partly for the bene
of the community, and partly let out to the heads
families for growing what each family needed. Eve
mission had its schools, which included instruction
agriculture and industrial arts, as well as in reading an
writing. It was, of course, necessary to protect the mi
sion from predatory individuals in the outside worl
and the missions were made closed social units, soci
islands, in which every contact with the world
getting and spending was carefully prevented.

It is impossible not to admire the idealism and th
noble credulity of these men, Dominicans, Franciscan
and Jesuits, who built up this mission life in Spanis
America. The influence of Las Casas was clearly pr
sent, for he had been convinced that the Indians po
sessed every natural virtue, except that they did n
know the truth, that is to say, the Gospel. Many of th
customs of the Indians—things which St Paul calle
"the beastly devices of the heathen"—were not sin, h
held, but merely ignorance of divine truth; and "t
give them opportunities of knowing that truth was th
only mission of the white man". The greatest inspire
of mission work of this kind was Vasco de Quirog
He incorporated women into the work of the grou
teaching them special crafts; and he made the Tarasca
Indians on the shores of Lake Pátzcuaro what they ar
to-day: the most useful Indian citizens of Mexic
Industrial arts, division of labour between one lak
side village and another, are only two of the things fo
which Tarascans remember the name of Don Vasco.

The Missions declined and disappeared because th
idea was as artificial as it was noble. It was no les
impossible to keep the Mission apart from the worl
than it was to keep the world away from Sanch
Panza's island.

The Portuguese in America

The history of Portuguese America is in many ways different from that of the Spanish possessions. Brazil was discovered by the Portuguese Admiral Cabral in 1500. Some say that the admiral was blown out of his course on the way to India and discovered Brazil by mistake; but it is more likely that the discovery of Brazil was a consequence of the studies of the group of Portuguese cosmographers whose researches had made possible the discoveries of the other great Portuguese navigators. In any case, Cabral formally took possession of the country which he had discovered, and sailed away to India round the Cape of Good Hope.

Portuguese rights in the New World had been established six years before by the Treaty of Tordesillas, after two vague and unsatisfactory attempts at settlement by the Borgia Spanish Pope, Alexander VI. By this treaty, the line of demarcation between the territory of Spain and Portugal was fixed 370 leagues west of the Cape Verde Islands, or roughly at longitude 50° West. The colonization of Brazil was at first left to private individuals, and was limited to a few small settlements on the coast. The Portuguese were more interested in the East Indies. Then, with the union of the crowns of Spain and Portugal under Philip II in 1581, all the European colonies in the world became possessions of the crown of Spain, and Portugal continued to be subject to the Spanish kings until 1640.

From the beginning, however, the Portuguese had taken a different view of their rights and obligations from that of the Spaniards. The colonists were inclined to sell everything they possessed in Portugal, and transport both themselves and their families to the New World. They preferred to think of an empire based on peaceful trading rather than one formed by conquest with

the avowed object of saving souls for the Church. "Th
Portuguese," Victoria told his pupils at Salamanca
"to their own great profit, have a big trade with
similar people [Indians], without reducing them to sub
jection." Yet from the beginning, Portuguese civiliza
tion in America was based on imported negro slaves
They succeeded in establishing the cane-sugar industry
and in a few years large stone houses—like medieva
castles—were being built near the tropical forests
These were the homes of the patriarchal families o
planters with their slaves. Along with intense in-breed
ing, which led to the creation of a powerful agrarian
aristocracy, there arose the mixed population described
in the first chapter. The Portuguese colonist of the six
teenth century "was like a Spaniard, without his mili
tant orthodoxy; like an Englishman, without his Purita
contours". He was daring, persistent, efficient; bu
seldom handicapped by inflexible principles, and thu
more adaptable than a Spaniard or an Englishman
He was from the beginning more cosmopolitan. From
the first he made himself notable for a certain power o
assimilation which set him apart from other European
of his time. The type of stone house that he develope
in Brazil was a combination of the manor house o
Portugal with the African and Asiatic buildings which
he had seen in Morocco, in China, in India, and in
Japan.

INDEPENDENCE

The story of Spanish American Independence ha
been told almost as often as that of the Conquest. Th
causes of the fall of the Spanish Empire are too comple
to be discussed here, but some of them have already
been indicated: the rigidity of the system and the hold
the mother country kept on colonies which were thou
sands of miles away. The Napoleonic invasion of Spain

808) and the flight of King Charles IV gave the
lonies their chance. In its results, independence was
anything a greater achievement than the conquest.
, too, produced outstanding figures: visionaries and
reamers who became leaders in war and politics and
'en adroit negotiators in obtaining help in Europe and
mpathy in the United States. The change, however,
as less than might have been imagined, in its effect
ı the lives of people in general. The rulers were no
nger Spaniards, officials representing the King of
pain, but creoles—men of Spanish origin born in
merica. The revolution was in substance a rising of
eoles against Spanish officials.

The curious thing was that the movement of revolu-
onary ideas became known in South America through
at class which, in Europe, was the object of all the
formers' attacks: the great landowners. Many of the
ns of rich colonials went to Europe for their education,
nd came back full of Voltaire, Rousseau, the Encyclo-
aedists, and Tom Paine. Such were Bolívar, San Mar-
n, O'Higgins, and Miranda. The course of the French
evolution forced liberal ideas on the attention of
panish colonials. British statesmen, Canning and
astlereagh in particular, also played a part in helping
ne Spanish colonies to secede; and there were many
ritish volunteers in the liberating armies; but British
on-intervention was of little importance compared with
ne achievement of Bolívar and San Martín.

The great fact still remains that their independence was won by the Latin Americans themselves.
It was their energy, courage, and persistence that
triumphed. It was their great leaders who saw the
way to overthrow the traditions of centuries. It was
their peoples who supplied the troops which over-
came the trained soldiers of Spain. The same is true
of Brazil, though the method was different. The
United States, despite the Monroe Doctrine, con-

> tributed hardly anything to the struggle while
> was in progress. . . . The work of Bolívar and S
> Martín . . . the greatness of their effort and t
> magnificence of many of their conceptions ha
> never been fully appreciated.[1]

Freedom was only won after prolonged milita operations over a vast stretch of country, converging the centre of the old Spanish empire, Peru. San Mar came up from Argentina and Chile (where he w joined by O'Higgins), while Bolívar came down fro Venezuela, Colombia, and Ecuador to complete t conquest of Peru and Bolivia. Many picturesque figu appeared on the scene, including the British admi Cochrane, who offered his services to the revolutiona cause, assembled a fleet of transports, and conveyed t liberating army of the Andes from Valparaiso to Lim

The liberation of the Spanish empire by Bolívar ar San Martín was a joint enterprise. Bolívar's ideal f South America had been a federation of all the Spani American States; the fact that they have settled dov into the separate countries of to-day has been due much to physical geography as to racial compositi and economic interests.

Bolívar, San Martín, Miranda, Egaña, and the rest- though their political ideals differed—were agreed up one point: the new States (they considered) were st unfitted for republican democracy. Bolívar was deep influenced by Montesquieu and Rousseau, and believ that "only democracy is susceptible of absolute liberty But all the constitutions which he sponsored provide for a strong executive. He even wondered whether might not be a good thing to try a constitution monarchy if a suitable monarch could be found. Sa Martín was less convinced than Bolívar of the virtues democracy; the republican government he desired w.

[1] C. K. Webster, *Great Britain and the Independence of La America* (Oxford, 1938).

LATIN AMERICA AS IT WAS—AND IS

(1) HOUSE IN GUAYAQUIL (ECUADOR) WHERE BOLÍVAR MET SAN MARTÍN
(Fox Photos)

(2) A STREET IN RIO DE JANEIRO (From the air)
(Mondiale, Ltd.)

one with a still stronger executive; and after the cel
brated meeting with Bolívar at Guayaquil, in Ecuado
he saw that they could never agree and withdrew
Europe.

The need for a strong executive has produced t
American president. He not only presides, he govern
He is the incarnation of national power and sovereignt
Ministers are responsible to him alone and can be d
missed by him; the man who governs is more importa
than the assembly of the people's representatives, for t
president, in himself, represents the people. In Euro
such a system would have led to unbridled dictatorshi
in the United States the constitutional checks on pres
dential power have so far proved sufficient. But
Spanish and Portuguese America, even in those repu
lics which have federal form and are described officia
as *estados unidos* (united states)—*e.g.*, Argentina, Braz
Chile, Mexico, Venezuela—there are constitutional pra
tices which may be used to limit or nullify the autonon
of the federal States; and means have been found f
keeping a president virtually, if not actually, in pow
for long terms, in spite of the constitutional safeguar
against re-election.

This constitutional supremacy of the president e
plains the natural propensity of Latin American gover
ments to relapse into dictatorship; and in fact many
the republics began with presidents who wielded almo
dictatorial powers: O'Higgins in Chile in 1818, Bolív
in Great Colombia in 1824; and particularly in Par
guay, the long dictatorship of Dr Francia (1814–4
which aroused the sympathy and admiration of Carlyl
Nowadays, if the president feels sure of the army
the air-force, he can defy the opposition or ignore i
The opposition in Latin America is generally persona
too, and stands less for an idea than for a man. There
immense prestige in the person of a party-leader; an

is often a general, a "headman" or *caudillo*,[1] like the esent ruler of Spain.

Though all the constitutions of Latin American States e democratic in form, there has been considerable riety in the practical working of democracy. Many fferent influences have affected American political nditions: the Declaration of Independence, the ench Revolution, and the reminiscences of old Spanish stitutions—*juntas*, *municipios*, *cabildos*, *ayuntamientos*—mparable with the self-governing elements of the old nglish village reproduced in New England.

In the United States, from the eighteenth century onwards, there was a relatively homogeneous people, sprung from Anglo-Saxon Europe. They were, in New England at any rate, protestants of Calvinist upbringing, living in religious societies and accustomed to manage their own affairs, whether they were the affairs of their Church or of their village, which indeed were practically the same thing. Such conditions naturally gave rise to a public opinion and a civic sense, the very foundations of democracy in the Anglo-Saxon sense of the word. Catholic Spaniards, on the contrary, in other parts of America, were jealously excluded by their clergy from any interference with the government of their Church; and Spain in the same way discouraged all aspirations towards autonomy in the sphere of administration or politics. Rather than a people, the Spanish colonists were the remains of an aristocracy—or rather, a conquering minority—dominating or exploiting a mass of Indians or mestizos. Under such conditions men remained individuals, in conformity with the old Iberian tradition, without ever becoming citizens. Their qualities remained personal to themselves, without ever developing into civic virtues; they never formed (like citizens of the United States) a

[1] The word is derived from *caput*, *capitellum*, "head", and has othing to do with *cauda*, "tail". A *caudillo* must always be at the ead of something.

> public opinion. In such barren social condition force naturally gained the upper hand, ar favoured the power of a leader who could make h presence felt, however doubtful (in a military c civil sense) his title might be.[1]

In some ways, society in Spanish America ha changed very little, least of all in the Andean region: and even where it has been most deeply affected by tl arrival of new immigrants—as in Argentina—the orig nal spirit may still be felt.

The conquistadores introduced, among a large India population where social development had not gor very far, a form of civilization which was feudal and a most static. In spite of independence—achieved (a already mentioned) mainly through the desire of tl creoles to free themselves from officials sent out fro: Spain—the social organization of the colonial epoch ha changed very little down to recent times. The creol remained the owners of vast properties, on which grou of Indians lived in exchange for the work they did c the estate. The foreign mine-owner recruited his labou by much the same means as the Spaniard. White me were left to govern a mixed assemblage of native race But in the last twenty years, in those countries in whic the proportion of Indians is large, the people of pu: Spanish descent (or those who could claim Spanis descent for two generations) have often been less tha 5 per cent. Their old preponderance has gone, and middle class, composed principally of mestizos, ha taken its place, and is demanding, with some of tl Indians, a larger share in the government of tl country.

The emancipation of the middle class is on the pr gramme of the *Aprista* movement (APRA: *Alian. Popular Revolucionaria Americana*), which came into exis

[1] André Siegfried, *Amérique Latine* (Paris, 1934).

BRAZIL

D

FISHING BOATS AT BAHIA
(*Paul Popper*)

IN RIO HARBOUR
(*Paul Popper*)

ence in Peru, in the University of Lima. "Let us not b
ashamed of calling ourselves Indo-americans" (*No n
avergoncemos de llamarnos indoamericanos*), the leader of th
movement, Sr. Haya de la Torre, has exclaimed in
recent manifesto. His movement has a pro-Indian ide
and aims at delivering Indo-america from foreign im
perialist exploitation, proclaiming the nationalizatio
of industry and calling for the separation of Churc
and State—already separate in some of the Lati
American countries. At the moment the directors
the movement are in exile, but their ideas are makin
progress.

Passing for a moment by the great experiment of th
Mexican Revolution (page 69) we find that in Braz
(November 1937) the form of government turned int
something which seemed to more than one observer t
have a somewhat sinister complexion. Perhaps thes
observers were mistaken; Portugal has done somethin
of the same kind, and its effort is admitted to be th
only tolerable solution so far provided for the probler
of the corporative state. But Brazil has had its ow
fascists, apart from those in the German and Italia
colonies which are not yet assimilated into the Brazilia
nation; and like the German and Italian groups, the
seem to have taken their orders from Europe. In view
of these dubious activities, President Vargas prohibite
all foreigners in Brazil from indulging in any politica
activity; but the nazi and fascist danger remains, i
Brazil and in some of the Spanish American countries
Communism has gained some ground in Chile, bu
elsewhere it is weak among the workers and hate
among the middle classes, both liberal and catholic.

Some writers have criticized the doctrinaire repub
licanism of South American revolutionaries; but doc
trinaire democracy has its importance, even as an un
realized ideal. In Latin America it has combined wit
nationalist feeling as a force against international foreig

:ploitation; and it has also determined sentiment—if
›t practice—in the present war. "Revolution" in
atin America really means reform and progress; it
›es not necessarily imply violence, and several of the
:ates have really achieved, or are beginning to achieve,
mething which may truly be called a democratic
›vernment. Further, democratic nationalism is, at the
oment, the only real force which may give the Indian
›pulation its chance.

"Nationalism" in Latin America to-day means a
:otest against non-Latin American interference; it is
›t a feeling dividing Latin American States from one
ıother. The twenty Latin American countries may,
.deed, be compared in a sense with ancient Greek
ties; they are not really foreigners to one another, in
›ite of their quarrels. An exile from one country nor-
ıally settles in another, and perhaps intrigues to get
ack—as Alcibiades did in Sparta. The Latin American
tates are, in fact, all members of one big family; and
r that reason, Latin America is one of the few regions
ı the world where disputes have been settled by
ıternational arbitration.

CHAPTER III

CONDITIONS OF LIFE

WHILE the European considers Latin America f
its mines and minerals, for investments or t
possibilities of immigration, the inhabitant
almost any Spanish or Portuguese American repub
considers his country as agricultural. *Quiero al campo,*
modern Uruguayan poet has said, *como todos los homb*
de América lo quieren (I love the country, as all the m
of Latin America love it). That is not a pose. Fro
the inhabitant of an Indian village, cultivating t
communally held village lands and trading by bart
to the owner of a large ranch or plantation, or
chilled-beef magnate in Buenos Aires, Latin Americ
life is still based on agriculture, as it has been for t
last four centuries.

ARGENTINA

Buenos Aires so dominates everything in Argenti
to-day that it is difficult to realize the existence of a
older Argentine culture in some of the provinces of t
interior, a culture which to some extent—and mor
perhaps, than is generally imagined—still affects li
and thought in the capital.

There is another difference between up-count
Argentines from the Chilean border and the inhabitan
of Buenos Aires: the difference in how their ancesto
came there. Unlike the creoles from up-country, t
citizens of Buenos Aires came by way of the Atlanti
while inland towns like Mendoza, Córdoba, Tucumá
had been settled from over the Andes and the Pacif
coast. In colonial times the Spanish Government

ome tried to make the transandine route the onl
getting goods into Argentina; the direct voyage
pain to Buenos Aires was forbidden. If a man in
uenos Aires had hides to sell, he was supposed to send
em overland all the way to Lima, ship them to
anama, convey them across the Isthmus, and from
ere ship them over to Spain. Barrels of imported
panish wine were supposed to come out by the same
ute. But generally they did not. A quicker way was
smuggling; and obliging Dutch and English smug-
ers were easily found to bring goods across the
tlantic to Buenos Aires and take creole hides and
ool in exchange. The object of this curious dispensa-
on of the home Government was the protection of
panish products from competition. Since the achieve-
ent of independence, several places in Chile and
endoza in the Argentine have been producing admir-
ble wines; but the Spanish colonial administration
ike the Emperor Domitian) destroyed the vines in its
ovinces. The same was the case with olive-growing
Mexico; the few surviving trees are all over 300
ars old.

The events of 1810 opened the port of Buenos Aires
foreign shipping. But before immigration could be-
n in earnest, the Pampa had to be freed of Indians.
l through the first half of the nineteenth century they
ade it dangerous to travel between Buenos Aires and
-country towns like Córdoba and Mendoza; and it
as not until General Roca had cleared the Indians
f the Pampa (1876) that it was worth while thinking
building railways.

The discovery of how to use the Pampa was a case
making the most of the opportunities offered by
ature.

It needed imagination, and the instinct of the agriculturalist . . . to see that the Pampa held

> treasures surpassing all the mines of precio metals in the world. On the Pampa, nature offer a vast field for agriculture and a vaster field f grazing. In the earliest Spanish days escaped catt and horses found abundant grasses to satisfy the hunger all the year round, for no winter sno covered the ground. . . . Presently creole an Spaniard discovered the new opportunity th nature thrust upon them, and took advantage it. In the good old days on the Pampa, in th days before the immigrant came, the *gaucho* w developed almost wholly by his environment. H was not a herdsman who cared for cattle, not breeder who improved the race, not a carefu owner who counted his herds and saw to the sustenance, but a hunter of horses and cows wh lived on an abundance that nature came very nea thrusting into his hands. The animals cared fo themselves. His occupation was the chase; h prey, the half wild cattle. He reacted to the en vironment truly. When they tell you to-day th the gaucho is extinct, they are thinking of him . . as a master of horse- and cattle-hunting, the ma who needed only a knife and a rope and th Pampa to provide himself with horses, cattl clothing, and food. There is no need for suc prowess now, nor has there been since steamers an railroads brought laboring men to the Pampa. I his quintessence the gaucho has long disappeared

He is still to be found, to a certain extent, but hardl the gaucho of legend; and in talking of these thing now with an Argentine or Uruguayan friend, on should remember that they belong, not to the preser of his country, but to the past; that they are far awa and long ago. While the gaucho lives on as a literar type, agriculture and scientific cattle-breeding hav spread a network of wire and railways across his ol country. In South America, railways led the move

[1] Mark Jefferson, *Peopling the Argentine Pampa* (America Geographical Society, Research Series, No. 16, 1926).

ient into unpopulated districts, while in the United tates they followed it. From agriculture have come ie immense grain and cattle exports; and with these ie importance of the Argentine Republic and the vealth of the Creole Argentine landowner.

Immigration into Argentina began slowly. From 810 to 1854 there was practically none. Agriculture vas virtually confined to the outskirts of towns, and it as been due to the continuous immigration of European farmers that the Argentine Pampa has become ne of the great granaries of the world. Between 1857 nd 1930 6,300,000 people of various nationalities migrated to Argentina.[1] They were mainly Italians nd Spaniards. Many did not become permanent ettlers, but returned to their own countries after trying he new one for a season or two; yet, on the whole, hose who stayed outnumbered those who went back. Not all of them were farmers, or tried their hand at arming. A large proportion settled in towns, and by 937 it was reported that urban industries needed at nost a few skilled workers, while the Argentine countryide was still empty. There were reasons for this. Agriultural colonization in Argentina had certain drawacks which had not been met with in the United tates, where those in search of land had had the hance of finding it cheap or even free. The immigrant n the Pampa found that there was no public land to e had, and that he had either to buy land for himself r rent it from an established landowner. Except for hose immigrants who settled in the agricultural colnies of Entre Ríos and Santa Fe, not many were able o become owners of their farms. As immigration inreased, land values rapidly went up; and landowners, ware of the rising value of their land, preferred to eep it and let others work it for them, rather than

[1] Isaiah Bowman, *Limits of Land Settlement* (New York: Council n Foreign Relations, 1937).

sell out to immigrants and invest their money in some-thing else. For this reason, there were, in 1937, estancias which would only let agricultural land for short periods and under certain conditions—*e.g.*, that the immigrant farmer would agree to sow alfalfa after he had grown two or three crops of wheat or maize. The reason was simple. From the point of view of the estancia, renting land to a farmer was only a means of obtaining a pasture of alfalfa, practically in-dispensable for fattening the cattle, on which the whole existence of an estancia depends.

Argentina is still mainly a country of large land-owners and tenant-farmers. There is no strong, united agrarian class, capable of becoming an element of economic progress and social well-being; in 1937 hired agricultural labourers were to be seen tramping the countryside looking for a day's work.[1] The problem was to transform the farm-labourer who had no capital beyond his tools and his work into an independent landowner—a problem which, since the depression of 1931, had become even more difficult; for the tenant farmer had never been able to put by enough to buy his farm.

The other great problem was to get the right type of immigrant that the country needed; and that could only be done if the economic prospects for the immi-grant were reasonably good. The Argentine Govern-ment was not one of those which welcomed immigrants from Republican Spain; and some might think that through this attitude a great opportunity was lost for Argentina. By 1937 the position was that if the Argen-tine Government could overcome the financial diffi-culties caused by the failure of private schemes of settle-ment—if (that is to say) they could find a sufficient number of large estates to be divided and at the same time check the activities of speculators in land—there

[1] Bowman, *loc. cit.*

'as still a limited outlook for further settlement on the ampa.

The southern part of Argentina—the Patagonian rovinces from the River Colorado down to the Straits f Magellan—were settled chiefly by people of English, cottish, Welsh, and Boer origin. It is mainly a poor, old country, thinly populated, the rainfall too small or farming, and the chief occupation of the settlers is aising cattle and sheep. Most of the land is owned by ie Government, though some people have established iemselves as squatters. Towns are practically con- ned to the Atlantic coast, and are occupied with the iipment of wool and frozen mutton. Railways are :w; and in 1937 it still took weeks for the long lines of 'ool-carts to reach the ports after shearing time.

BRAZIL

Brazil was originally appropriated by colonists from ortugal, Holland, and France, who fought for the ight to remain in the enormous territory then recently iscovered. Bands of explorers gradually worked their 'ay into the interior. They went forward like the tribes the Bible, with their families, their priests, their idges, and their generals.[1]

The economic history of Brazil has developed in a :ries of "single-crop cultures". For a time they domi- ated the markets of the world, and then failed under ie competition of intensive cultures which arose in ther parts of the world, and succeeded because they 'ere better organized. Each of these single-crop cul- ıres coincided with the advance of the economic fron- .er and the development of a new area, and even a ew type of civilization; and each new development nded in a crisis produced by competition elsewhere.

[1] Alfonso Reyes, *Homilia por la cultura* (Mexico: Fondo de cultura :onómica, 1938).

The chief stages have been sugar, gold, cotton, rubbe and coffee.

Sugar-cane was first brought to Brazil from Madeir in 1532; and up to the end of the seventeenth centur Brazilian sugar was leading the market. The Dutc colonists of Pernambuco (or Recife) lived by suga and when they left in 1655, sugar sank to the level c a domestic industry. There were, however, othe reasons for the decline. From the middle of the sever teenth century, gold and diamond mines had begun t attract labour and capital to other parts of Brazil planters and their slaves migrated to Minas Geraes c Rio de Janeiro. Yet the production of sugar still wer on, in spite of competition—the most serious bein the development of beet-sugar in Europe; and thoug the construction of railways tended to convert the smal widely scattered plantations into great concerns, th abolition of slavery (1888) left the industry withou labour. The war of 1914–18 brought a period of partia prosperity, and Brazil still produces enough sugar fo its own use; while coffee (which Brazilians drink ver sweet) helps to keep up the demand for sugar. Th new industry of preserved fruit also brings suga considerable benefit.

In the eighteenth century Brazilian industry wa dominated by gold. The mines, though discovere earlier, only became profitable to work after som lucky prospecting in 1693. So many adventurer joined in the gold-rush that a considerable cattle industry came into existence to feed them. Europea capital first made its appearance in 1824, and a con siderable portion of the gold of Brazil found its way t England. Portuguese debts (especially to Britain) wer transferred to the account of Brazil. On the return c the Royal Family to Portugal, most of the liquid asset of the Brazilian Treasury went too, with the result tha in Brazil, crisis followed crisis throughout the nineteent entury, and it is said that old parrots may still be ought which will talk of nothing but a bank which roke in the sixties of the last century. Finally, in 1918, he export of gold was prohibited.

Cotton had only a comparatively short run in Brazil —from the end of the eighteenth century to the end of he Civil War in the United States—but it is still an mportant crop. Rubber experienced a boom during he war of 1914–18, though it has not been able to hold ts own against the variety cultivated in the Malay tates, grown originally from seeds smuggled out of Brazil by an Englishman.

Coffee has been the last and most important example n Brazil of the single-crop system. Since no harvest an be expected in less than five years, more capital is eeded, and a new type of planter has come into existnce, one who is at the same time a city business man.

From its size, which is approximately equal to that f the United States, Brazil has come to be regarded as he land of opportunity; but the proportion of immirants who afterwards return to their mother countries s a warning that many of them do not find everything o their liking. Even after fifty years of immigration on large scale, the country still has an enormous amount f undeveloped, fertile land in regions in which Europeans can become acclimatized. Many thousands, robably, would be only too glad of a bare subsistence, f they were allowed to say good-bye to Europe and stablish themselves permanently in Brazil, on almost ny terms. From the Brazilian point of view, however, he establishment of immigrants in such primitive onditions would contribute nothing to the economic rosperity of the country and would hamper social rogress.[1]

In the south-west of Brazil is a thousand-mile belt of rassland and mixed forest on the upper reaches of the

[1] Bowman, *loc. cit.*, p. 320.

rivers Paraguay and Paraná. Though this stretch o
country is shared by four Governments—Argentina
Brazil, Bolivia, and Paraguay—most of it lies in Brazilian
territory, and it is here that there is the greatest promis
for future settlement. The climate, however, has to b
considered. In latitudes between 16° and 23° South
people of white race find the climate somewhat trying
even if they live from 900 to 3000 feet above th
sea.

Settlements are also creeping across the still un
explored—or only partially explored—region to th
west of S. Paulo: the Sertão. To form a settlement
the forest must be cleared of undergrowth and smalle
trees, and the wood burnt just before the rains begin
The first crop is maize, which is fed to the half-wil
pigs. After a year or so, the settler begins to plan
coffee; but enough room has to be cleared for th
coffee-bush to feel what is locally called "the breat
of the forest". Coffee is the most important crop; bu
since the soil is rapidly exhausted, the chief coffee-
producing centres are constantly moved westwards
and the policy has been to establish new plantation
rather than keep up the old ones. A limit to the production of coffee was set by the restriction laws o
1928; and the colonists had to try other crops, such a
rice, grown with great success by Japanese settlers,
and wheat and rye raised by German settlers who fled
to Brazil to escape persecution by the Nazis. The
German settlements farther to the South have main-
tained most of their national characteristics; but their
children were said, a few years ago, to be losing to
some extent their German speech, in spite of the schools
of which the colonists are justly proud.

The great centre for Japanese colonization in Brazil
is the hot, moist, coastal region, south-west of Santos.
Farm-buildings, fields, crops, have all been copied from
those in Japan. The colony is large (173,500 in 1927),

COUNTRY LIFE

(1) ARGENTINE CATTLE (From the air)
(*Mondiale, Ltd.*)

(2) SUN AND SHADOW IN ECUADOR
(*Fox Photos*)

and some 40 per cent. are employed on coffee plar tations.

On the central Brazilian plateau, the higher peak provide summer pasture, and even sometimes show few degrees of frost. This mountain zone is inhabite by small farmers. Italians have built up vineyards and the district, which a hundred years ago was empty is now one of the most populous parts of souther Brazil.

Chile

Chile is essentially an agricultural country. To th outer world it is best known for its minerals—in par ticular, nitrates and copper—but it is not in workin these that most of the population is employed. Chil is a good example of what went on generally in Spanis America in colonial times. The agrarian system of th Spanish American colonies, though it came into exis ence more or less by accident, soon followed a wel regulated procedure, with a precise method of acquirin and holding land; and the property acquired and hel in this way led to the great *haciendas*, so characteristi of Spanish American colonies, which existed in Mexic down to the agrarian reforms of recent times an still exist in Chile to-day.

The following is a description of a visit to a hacienda situated in the Aconcagua Valley, abou forty miles north of Santiago.

> He drove us . . . along a country road line with Lombardy poplars, now bright yellow in th late May days of autumn. Then, entering the farı through a gate in a high mud wall, we followe through avenues of eucalyptus, poplar and weep ing willow a couple of miles by a round-abou road to the house. Most of the land we saw wa in alfalfa, with cattle and horses grazing its shor cropped growth. We passed a few fields of grai

and saw well-kept vineyards rising row on row along the foot of the hills as far up the slope as canals could supply them with water. Each individual field was enclosed by rows of tall poplars, the red roots of the trees exposed along the half-filled irrigation ditches. Long lines of weeping willows too bordered some of the plots. The house was a one-storey structure of some twenty rooms. It had thick adobe walls and a tile roof. . . . It stood in the midst of gardens occupying several acres and filled with flowers and fruit and ornamental trees. It was built around several *patios*, or enclosed courts, as are most of the older houses in Chile, each of these open to the sky and paved with tile or cobble-stones. Potted plants stood about these spaces, while a small fountain and pool occupied the center of the principal court. The rooms opened on long covered porches which surrounded these patios on all four sides.[1]

The country is well favoured for irrigation. The deep owdrifts which winter leaves on the Andes store the ater, and give it off gradually during the warmer onths. On the lower slopes, up to about 10,000 feet, e snow melts quickly on the approach of spring; it above that height it lies in deep drifts throughout e year. These make great frozen reservoirs, giving a irly constant flow of water to something like twenty nall rivers which cross central Chile to the sea, and which the largest is the Bio-Bio in the south, for long e frontier between the Spaniards and the Araucanian id Mapuche Indians.

Central Chile is a comparatively small region—a tle smaller than England and Scotland combined—d much of it is unsuited for human habitation. The rtile part is the central valley which lies between the wering peaks of the Andes and the rounded slopes of e Coast Range; and this central district, with its ex-

[1] MacBride, *Chile: Land and Society* (American Geographical ciety, Research Series, No. 19, 1936).

ceptionally fertile soil, has been occupied by whites f
nearly 400 years. It is a country of large estates, wi
the landowner's house far away from the road and t
humble brown hut of the labourer (*inquilino*) hard
see.

Chile, down to very recent times, has been a "tw
class society". If there is a dash of Indian blood
both classes, the mixture occurred so long ago that t
modern Chileans do not reveal the atavism of mix
breeds. They are virtually a new race, and a ve
attractive one, with definite, transmissible characte
istics, betraying no tendency to revert to either of t
ancestral stocks.[1] There has also been an admixtu
of English and Irish: Edwards, Walker, William
Tupper, Clark, Holly, Miller, Thompson, Lync
Carey, Cochrane, Mackenna, O'Brien, are all famili
names; while the founder of Chilean independen
O'Higgins, was the son of a Viceroy of Peru who w
an Irishman from County Meath.

Visitors from the United States often find Sou
Americans more European than themselves. In Ch
particularly they observe an acknowledged upper cl
assuming the privileges as well as the responsibilities
a landed aristocracy; while the peasant accepts his i
feriority. He still lives in primitive conditions with
nominal wage, the use of an acre or two of land,
wretched hut of unbaked bricks, the privilege of usi
some animals from the farm, and the almost feud
obligation to serve all the needs of his master's hou
For this he receives fatherly advice, care in sickne
medicine and personal attention, and help and prote
tion in special adversity; but it can hardly be sa
that the present system in Chile has worked we
"It is all in absolute contrast with development in t
United States, where none of the native-born have a

[1] Mark Jefferson, *Recent Colonization in Chile* (American G
graphical Society Research Series, No. 6, 1921).

nse of inferiority, except of a temporary character."[1] hile is said to be the poorest country in Latin merica per head of the population.

There is no doubt that in Chile the hacienda stem made for stability in the past; and this favoured conomic progress and set Chile apart as one of e most settled countries in America. "Chile broke way from Spain," it has been said, "but not from panish institutions"; it achieved independence without revolution. There was a transfer of authority, but ot a political reformation, and less social disturbance an in any other country in Latin America. The aders of the revolt were almost all landowners, *acendados*; and the war of independence in Chile was ought by one set of landowners against another. That as not quite what O'Higgins had in mind. He had reamed of making Chile a real democracy, and in the arly years of the Republic he worked hard for liberal nd educational reform. Yet any advance in this direction was made in spite of the large landowners; and e power of this oligarchy, which had dominated Chile r over a hundred years, ended only in 1927. "It now," says MacBride, "a choice between agrarian reorm or revolution. Only a fundamental modification f the hacienda system with its inquilinos (the labourers n the estate) can save the country (and the hacendados emselves) from a disaster such has befallen the hacendados of Mexico, who were too blind to reform themelves; for, like their opposite numbers in Mexico thirty ears ago, they are faced by the alternative of giving p part of their lands voluntarily, without compensaon, or of losing them entirely."

Chile, a country over 2600 miles long, extending om the tropics to Cape Horn, can naturally show xtremes of climate. While in the northern nitrate eserts "one passes browns and yellows day after day,

[1] Mark Jefferson, *loc. cit.*

unrelieved by the smallest patch of green", in t
southern forest district of heavy rainfall, for 900 mi
the woods are so wet that it is impossible to start a fi
for clearing, without constant relighting, even when
the people of the countryside turn out to help.[1] On t
island of Chiloé, at the south margin of the for
settlement, the problem is to maintain any clearing
the forest at all. Settlement is practically limited to t
fringe. Foreigners as well as Chileans have taken pa
in the work of colonization: Germans, Swiss, Englis
French, and Spanish. There is no longer any gre
possibility of occupying land; but the frontier regi
needed settlement, and both socially and economical
has been of great value to the Chilean nation. T
extreme southern part of Patagonia and the Straits
Magellan also belong to Chile, and Chileans are i
creasing there, although it is 1200 miles from t
capital. The houses look Chilean, and Chileans for
the majority of the workers. Large businesses, howeve
are chiefly in the hands of foreigners: British, Yug
slavs, Germans, or Spaniards. Here, as at Llanquih
farther north, the Chilean feels like an alien in his ow
country, and complains that foreigners are taking aw
the wealth of the land; yet Chileans come to seek in t
far south the independence which they cannot find
central Chile where the land is still held by relative
few owners.

Mexico

The population of Mexico is for the most part
village population;[2] very few families live in lone
farms. The villages are places out of which people go t

[1] M. Jefferson, *The Rainfall in Chile* (American Geographic
Society, Research Series).

[2] R. Redfield, *Tepoztlan: a Mexican Village* (Chicago Universi
Press, 1930).

ork and into which they go to trade. The men scatter
tside the village to perform their daily tasks, whether
ey own their fields (*milpas*) or not; some of them work
mills, or in mines still farther away, returning at the
d of the day, the week, or the season. But while the
llagers live by agriculture, the village lives by trade.
is essentially a market; and the central *plaza* is the
ace for the regular markets attended by people from
her villages round, as well as the site of public build-
gs and private dwellings of any size or importance.
nere is a social distinction between those who live in
e centre of the village, on or near the market-place,
d those who only dwell in the outskirts.

> Tepoztlan is very good to look at. Here are some 700 houses—the total population is 4000 souls—arranged along little shaded streets, many of them bowered in flowers. Flowers are more important to Mexicans than are motor-cars, radios and bathtubs combined, to Americans. The houses are small and very simple. Their walls are of adobe brick, sometimes whitewashed; their roofs are of red tile or of thatch; they have no chimney, frequently no windows, no glass; very little woodwork. In the front yard stands the circular corncrib made of cornstalks [bound together with rope], precisely as it stood in the days of Montezuma; behind there is often a vegetable garden. There may be a shed for horse, cow or burro, while turkeys, chickens, and pigs wander introspectively over the foreground. Dogs invariably take their siestas in the street. As why should they not? Wheeled vehicles are unknown.[1]

A picture of the industrial life of Mexico would have to
clude the 70,000 little Indian communities scattered
roughout rural Mexico and living in many places
most outside the national economy. What is true
Mexico is true of Guatemala and large parts of other

[1] Stuart Chase, *Mexico: a study of two Americas* (London, 1932).

Central American republics, and of wide areas Bolivia, Paraguay, Ecuador, and Peru, much of Braz and even parts of Chile.

> There is, first of all, the primitive economy of t "uncivilized" Indian groups—nomads, with sense of private ownership, who play no rôle in t monetary economy of the country, yet who occu a large area. . . .
>
> Secondly, there are the communal and sem communal villages. These comprise a large pr portion of the rural population of the country. Th are largely self-sufficient, largely outside the schen of economic life that is dependent upon mon as a base. They grow their own food, build th own homes, largely make their own clothing, b . . . and sell very little. They are only in t slightest degree organized in terms of moneta economy. . . .
>
> There is, thirdly, the economy of the lar plantation. This plantation, unless it is located the coast and is dedicated to an exportable cr like bananas or coffee, is generally operated wi little reference to monetary terms. The position the labourers on the plantation is governed tradition and ancient rule, the wages, if any a paid, are likely to be in kind, or through a con missary which converts a nominal money wage in a payment in kind. The contracts are made crop shares without any money equivalents, t income of the plantation owner may be regulat in terms of a specified amount of crop to delivered by the manager, or a specified amount money which has no direct bearing upon t actual productivity of the plantation. . . . T economy of the Mexican plantation was up to 19 and, in a measure, to this date is still, on a no monetary basis. . . .
>
> There is, further, the economy of the small market town which though more nearly related the scheme of money values, still lives by bart The Indians exchange in the stores the things th

bring for the things they wish to take away, and the storekeeper exchanges the things he receives—pottery, blankets, hats, sandals—for other things that Indians from other villages bring—corn (maize), wheat, agricultural products, chickens. These in turn are retailed among the population of the village for labor in carrying, transporting, or other labor. While money plays a rôle here, it is a minor rôle rather than a major one. . . .[1]

The Spaniards found the Indians living under a :ll-defined system of land-tenure; but the 300 years Spanish dominion were characterized by persistent 'orts to concentrate the land in the hands of a few eat landholders. The growth of the large hacienda ıs due to the political and economic results of the nquest; its purpose seems to have been one of security ther than profit, and it strove to be as nearly self-fficient as possible.[2] The first break in the tendency concentrate landholding in Mexico among a few nilies came at the beginning of the nineteenth cen-ry; but all attempts to destroy the quasi-feudal aracter of the Mexican land-system were defeated by e policy of Porfirio Díaz during his thirty years' esidency, which only ended in 1910. This was olently upset during the revolution which overthrew n.

It is difficult to appreciate a movement as complex d many-sided as the Mexican Revolution. The forces play were not all on the surface. The battles were t the whole history of the Revolution; nor were the rious actors who played their parts, with more or less urance, on the various stages; and if some were ere gangsters, others were perfectly honest and sin-re, and earned the respect even of those who lost erything. "Poor Sr. Madero!" Even those who have

Frank Tannenbaum, *Whither Latin America?* (New York, 34).
Frank Tannenbaum, *The Mexican Agrarian Revolution*, 1930.

most cause to deplore his actions, have been heard refer in this way to the gentle spirit who dared to sta up to Díaz, and so began the Revolution. A civil war i fearful thing to have in one's own country.

With all its courage, with all its devotion, with all failings, and with all its horrors, the Revolution h brought a profound and beneficent change—a chan both spiritual and social—which has deeply affected t lives and thoughts of all Mexican citizens. Yet it wou never have come to be the great chapter it is in t history of the country without the tenacity and pers tence of some of its leaders, including Zapata. It is n enough to dismiss Zapata as a gunman or brigand, w burnt country houses and held up people in their ca Though Zapata was eventually trapped and killed, l doctor was made the governor of a State, and a *Zap tista* general was given a command in the regular arm Zapata won, and so did the Revolution, because would make no compromise over his simple demand land for the people.

> The Mexican Revolution began seven yea earlier than the Russian. It is as distinct fro communism as President Vargas' *Estado Novo* Brazil is different from fascism. It is entirely Me can, the product of Mexican history and Mexic conditions, and to identify this remarkable expe ment with communism is to fall into a confusion thought.[1]

The spiritual change brought by the Revolution best seen in the new attitude towards the Indian; a in the discovery of the country as well as the city—t country with its sharply different culture, its gre variety of life, its needs, and its poverty. The count has become a matter of concern to the Mexican Gover ment in a way it never was before; and the discovery

[1] R. A. Humphreys, *Latin America* (Oxford Pamphlets on Wo Affairs, No. 43, 1941).

ıe country means the transition from a colonial .entality to pride in a national State. Mexico has :come a nation because the whole of the country is .cluded in the political consciousness of its new rulers. 'ntil then, the relation of Mexico City to the rest of the ›untry had been that of a foreign government to a ›lony.

The Revolution brought ruin to the old ruling class; weakened the political and economic power of the hurch, awakened a feeling of national pride and racial ›nsciousness, gave power to labour, and abolished eonage. But all these changes depended on the altered ›cial structure brought by the change in the land-'stem; and the final effect of the Revolution will ıly be judged by its effect on the Mexican hacienda. 'he hacienda has been the most characteristic of the ıstitutions brought by the Spanish conquest, and the ıost unyielding. It was an estate, often as large as a nall principality in Europe, with stone walls running ›r mile after mile as far as the eye could see. There was big house somewhere in the middle—a sort of castle, ırrounded by a high wall, with the miserable huts of ıundreds of peons round about it.

The peon was born on the plantation and died on it, and from his birth to his death all of his activities fell within the sphere of his master's dominion. He was born into debt, because the children inherited their parents' obligations. He acquired a debt in his own right at baptism, because the cost of the *fiesta* it occasioned was advanced by the *hacendado* and money was borrowed for the priest, for the *aguardiente* ["fire-water," spirit]. His first clothes—made from white *manta*—were purchased from the plantation store, the *tienda de raya*, against his future wage. When he was old enough to marry, money for the festivities was borrowed from the plantation owner; when children were born, the same process led to the same

> end—further debt. The religious holidays wer celebrated with borrowed money, sickness wa marked by dependence upon the *patrón* for th payment of such medication as was to be had; an when the peon died he was buried with such hono drink, prayer and festivity as money borrowed fro the same source made possible. . . .
>
> The wage received—a nominal wage[1]—wa largely paid in kind. . . . The peon could not leav because he had nowhere to go. There were stat where the peon could find a change of master onl by finding a purchaser, that is, by finding someon who would take over his debt. It was in th way that the first labor for the railroads wa gathered. . . .
>
> The plantation was Mexico. It paid few taxe It built no roads. It imported nothing from ou side, and exported next to nothing. It made n effort to improve the tillage, the tools, the crops c the lives of its dependents. It was not an economi institution, it was a political one.[2]

It is still early to see what the effects of the ne Mexican land-policy are likely to be; nor is it clear wh will be the consequence of the action against the foreig oil companies. The Revolution aimed above all a regaining, for the benefit of Mexicans themselves, th resources of their country which had been exploited b foreigners. The stand against the oil companies was th great test of its sincerity. In Chile the Governme could afford to sit still and collect the substanti royalties paid over by the foreign concerns engaged i the export of nitrates. In Mexico a vital commodity lik oil could not be treated in that way, and protracte negotiations, carried out with obstinacy on one side an intransigeance on the other led, in March 1938, to th

[1] Agricultural wages had not risen since 1792. R. Humphrey *loc. cit.*, p. 21.

[2] Frank Tannenbaum, *Peace by Revolution: an Interpretation Mexico* (Columbia University Press, 1933).

‹propriation of seventeen companies, British and 'nited States. By the Mexican nation this act is re-ırded as a new Declaration of Independence; but the ›mpanies persist in describing it as mere robbery, ıough they have never denied the theoretical right of ıe Government to expropriation. Actually, more oil 'as produced in the first months of Government control ıan the representatives of the companies would have elieved possible; but the smooth working of the ıdustry was not achieved at once, and occupied the ›nstant attention of President Cárdenas. Expro-riation led to a rupture of diplomatic relations with ·reat Britain and a British boycott of Mexican oil. .elations have now happily been restored, but any ›mpromise on the oil question remains, for Mexico, a olitical impossibility.

URUGUAY

Though Uruguayans feel themselves to be—and are— : the opposite extreme to Mexicans in many respects, :t a remark by a former president of Uruguay, José atlle, would be fully endorsed in Mexico. "From the oint of view of national economy", he said, "a waste-ıl administration by the State is always preferable to ıe efficient management of an industry by foreign ıterprise."[1] It was found in Uruguay that the ·reigner's efficiency merely increased the amount of the ividends sent abroad, without affecting domestic ıdustry; while the State, though sometimes guilty of nploying too large a staff and of paying excessively igh wages, added by so doing to purchasing power at ome.

Uruguay had been like the country of an Homeric ing, with innumerable sheep and cattle like the Cattle

[1] S. G. Hanson, *Utopia in Uruguay* (Oxford University Press: ·ew York, 1938).

of the Sun. But about 1900 came the *frigorífico* (frozen meat factory). For something like twenty years th Argentine breeders had been trying to break dow European prejudice against frozen meat; the Boer Wa helped to put the industry on its feet. It sent up th price of livestock, and the result was that instead of be ing bred for wool, the flocks were now bred for size an flavour. But they took some time to reach the highe standard required for chilled beef, in comparison wit frozen; and it was chilled beef, more perishable tha frozen but selling at a higher price, that the stockme were after. In the war of 1914, the trade in chille beef was practically destroyed by the unreliability c the shipping service, due to naval action in the Atlanti Exporters had to rely chiefly on frozen beef, while th demand for tinned "bully" beef became ten times wha it had been before. The war-boom collapsed, howeve in 1920, and since then there has been considerabl antagonism to the foreign-owned *frigoríficos* while th present war has brought the country fresh economi difficulties.

In Uruguay there is hardly any waste land: 87 pe cent. is productive, either for grazing or agricultur the wooded areas are only 3 per cent. of the who country—less than any other country in South Americ There is a good rainfall in six years out of seve evenly distributed throughout the year, and it is th which produces the nutritious grasses and permits ope grazing at all seasons so that Uruguay ranks second t Argentina among the world's leading exporters of bee The well-drained pasture-lands are also suitable fo sheep-raising, and the countryside shows all the featur of twentieth-century pastoral life. It is not a tropic country, but has an ideal temperate climate, and the are no Indians.

Uruguay, of all the countries in South America, probably the most friendly to Britain. Uruguaya ke to remember British help and encouragement t difficult moments in their struggle for independnce—not so much against Spain, as against two nuch larger and more powerful neighbours, Argentina nd Brazil. They also think gratefully of the beneficial ffect of British pedigree stock on their flocks and ıerds. Their country is well-governed, well-run from he point of view of local government, and they are articularly well-educated. Primary, secondary, and igher education are provided by the State free of harge, so that the humblest Uruguayan citizen is vithin reach of the highest branches of learning, and at o cost to himself. The State provides everything; there re no fees for matriculation, or examinations, nor any harge for attending classes, laboratories, or hospitals. t is a country which, though it looks to the future, still unlike some of its neighbours) looks towards Europe, nd is close to Europe—to the Europe which used to nean Western civilization.

. . . . .

Prospects for the Future

Emphasis has been laid on country life and agriultural development, because the resources of Latin merica are not well-placed for the future development of heavy industry—indeed, they are situated so as o make any great industrial development very difficult. Chile has some deposits of iron as well as coal, but they re not very extensive; while even in Brazil—which has ne of the largest deposits of iron in the world, and great deal of water-power which might be converted nto electricity—the absence of coal would probably inder any great development of steel manufacture n that country. This holds good also for Argentina, Jruguay, and Paraguay; and it means that the development of heavy industry in these countries could onl take place on imported steel and imported coal. Th great mineral wealth of some of the other countries— the tin, zinc, and lead of Bolivia, for instance—will no help; and the question whether South America wil ever become industrialized remains to be answered.

In Central America there are practically no in dustrial resources at all; while in the islands, the iro deposits in Cuba are being exported to the Unite States. The small deposits of coal in Mexico are un likely to lead to any greater industrial developmen there than there is at present.

Since the depression of 1930, however, Latin Americ has turned in self-defence to such industrialization as i can, and has been investing its domestic capital i domestic manufacturing.

> Brazil developed a textile industry sufficient no only for her own needs but such as to cause con cern to Manchester exporters to Argentina Argentina made great strides in the manufacture o cottons and woollens, and became self-sufficient i the domestic supply of boots and shoes. Industria activity in Chile increased rapidly, and it has bee estimated that probably about one-third of th gainfully employed population is now engaged i industry. . . .[1]

These developments were accompanied by the growt of a new middle class, and customs became more thos of an industrialized, capitalistic society. Efforts wer made to control foreign trade and foreign capital Governments endeavoured to buy out foreign interests and in the face of a new economic nationalism foreig investors found their profits declining. In old day the industrial concerns in Latin America which ha been developed by foreign capital were mostly ru

[1] R. A. Humphreys, *Latin America* (Oxford, 1941).

SPANISH COLONIAL ARCHITECTURE

(1) A TWO-STOREYED CLOISTER

(2) PORCH OF THE CATHEDRAL, QUITO

on a concession basis. In England, the capital for suc
concerns (*e.g.*, a tramway company or a water-work
would be provided by a body of shareholders, ofte
local people, who had some control over the policy
the undertaking. With a concession, however, the co
cessionaire continues to hold the property and control
as long as the concession lasts, in the interests of foreig
shareholders thousands of miles away; while the loc
people have no say in the matter, though they have
accept the service provided by the holders of th
concession. Two examples may be given of the inco
venience caused by these foreign-planned and foreign
owned means of communication. A railway map
South America (such as that given in *The Republics*
South America), shows tracks of four different gauge
broad-gauge (5 ft. 6 in.), standard (4 ft. 8½ in.), met
(3 ft. 3 in.), and narrow (less than a metre). I
one or two cases (such as the high mountain section
the Transandine railway from Mendoza to Valparais
the difference in gauge is justified; but in most in
stances (such as the tracks radiating from Bueno
Aires across the Pampa) the only reason for the exi
tence of three different gauges must be that differen
countries have supplied the material, and seem to hav
insisted on the Argentines taking the kind of materi
which they found it most convenient to supply.

> The existing gauge-confusion began because th
> first locomotive on the Buenos Aires Western Rai
> way was an English one (built for a broad-gaug
> track in India, diverted for use in the Crimea
> War, and then bought second-hand for Argentin
> while French one-metre gauge equipment wa
> bought for more northerly lines.[1]

Uruguay, in this respect as in some others, stand
alone; when railways began to be built in the 1870'

[1] *The Republics of South America*, 44.

THE LEGACY OF SPAIN

(1) BELFRIES OF EL TEJAR, QUITO

(2) TOWER OF LA MERCED, FROM THE CLOISTER

a plan was drawn up for the whole Republic, and all t
lines are of the same standard gauge.

Something of the inconvenience produced by
confusion of gauges is found with the foreign-own
telephones in Mexico City. There are two differe
companies: Ericsson and Nacional. It is impossible
know off-hand which system the subscriber you wa
will be on; and many people are on both systen
having to pay installation-charges, hire, and rent to t
two different companies for two different instrumen
which do not work in quite the same way and ha
systems of numbers which are not unlikely to get cc
fused. The only thing the two systems have in comm
(it is said) is that the shareholders of the two compan
are practically the same.

Such confusion, which would hardly be tolerated
Europe (let alone in the United States) shows h
tiresome it can be to have public utilities in forei
hands.

Industrialization in Latin America is yet only in
beginnings, and its future is problematical. But it
already causing a change in the basis of the relations
Latin America with the rest of the world. Not all
these States have yet attempted to break down a colon
economy; but what is taking place in Latin Ameri
to-day has been called "a declaration of econon
independence".

There is one other type of industry in Latin Ameri
which has generally been neglected by economis
the village industry recorded by folklorists or anth
pologists. For understanding a country—let alone
continent—the simplest human activity is as importa
in its way as the most complicated. Both may be at t
same time economics, folklore, anthropology—and a
poetry. In Lima, till lately, many things were sold in t
streets, and the street criers used to come round
different times of the day. The last was the *jazmine*

SPANISH FORMS AND INDIAN FANCIES

(1) ALTAR IN CHURRIGUERESQUE STYLE CARVED BY INDIANS (QUITO)

(2) SAN FRANCISCO: A TYPICAL CHURCH IN QUITO

the jasmine-seller, at 5 p.m. He would shout: "*¡ Jard*
jardín! Muchacha, ¿ no hueles?" ("Gardens! Garden
Missy, don't you smell 'em?")

Latin America can only really be understood by tho
who can appreciate the poetry as well as the economi
the *jazminero* of Peru as well as the *frigorífico* of Urugua

CHAPTER IV

LITERATURE AND THE ARTS

LITERATURE and the arts—architecture, sculpture, painting, and music—did not begin in America with the arrival of the Spaniards and Portuguese. here had been architecture before they came; but uch of it was destroyed through the military neces- ities of the conquest. The Venetian canals of Mexico ity were filled in, choked by the rubble of the Indian ouses; churches arose on the ruins of pagan temples. et the battered fragments of the old gods—particu- rly the Plumed Serpent—were built into the new hurches; old idols were kept behind new altars and autiously brought out when the catholic priest was not ere. The old religion was not dead; and fears that it ight revive accounted for the destruction of most of e Aztec records in picture-writing. But some of the panish friars were also scholars, like Padre Sahagún; nd they were able to save a considerable quantity of ndian tradition, as well as material for the study of ndian language; historians of Indian religion, like . Mendieta, noticed the extraordinary likeness be- ween some of the Mexican myths and the Christian erities.

Yet if the old religion survived under a new form, so id the Indian races. The Spaniards showed no aver- on from Indian women, or the Portuguese from negro aves. The first modern Mexican was the son of stout ortés and his Indian interpreter, Doña Marina, and e was afterwards suspected of plotting independence om Spain; while by the third generation most of the escendants of the conquistadores had Indian grand- others.

The first American writer, the Inca Garcilaso de l
Vega, was the son of a cousin of a Spanish poet know
all over Europe and a daughter of the Inca roya
family. His *Comentarios reales* give a magnificent de
scription of Peru, with a record of the legends, laws
beliefs, ceremonies, and sufferings of a civilized people
suddenly and unexpectedly made vassals of Spain
But the traditions recorded by the Inca Garcilaso i
Peru, like those gathered by Padre Sahagún in Mexico
were regarded as dangerous. In the eighteenth centur
the Council of the Indies prohibited the reading of th
Comentarios reales, for its subversive tendencies; whil
Sahagún's documents remained unpublished until th
nineteenth century. The study of Indian traditio
was so firmly discouraged by the vested interests c
planters and officials, that after 1600 it disappeared
and only modern scholars have been able to read suc
things as the hymns to the old gods or the Aztec accour
of the capture of Mexico—a tale which moves us in th
same way as Virgil's account of the capture of Troy
because (like the *Aeneid*) it is an old story, told from th
other side.

Latin America can claim the first printing-press o
the American continent, as well as the earliest uni
versities. Printing began in Mexico in 1539; whil
three-quarters of a century before Harvard there wer
universities at Santo Domingo, Mexico, and Lima
Unfortunately the activities of both Press and Universit
were hampered by oppressive regulations, ecclesiastica
and civil; and in the end neither institution did a
much for literature and learning as might have bee
hoped for from their promising beginnings.

The record of discovery, conquest, and exploration i
so extraordinary that it would be mere pedantry not t
include among the first American writers Cortés an
the other conquistadores who settled in America an
wrote histories or reminiscences. Their writings have

uality that is all their own, a quality which gives them mperishable interest, in spite of faults of grammar, tyle, or accuracy. Even the stiff periods of Cortés, vell suited to writing to an Emperor, sometimes allow im to drop to a confidential tone of modesty or even amiliarity; and in a moment of emergency he will eap on to a horse and carry you straight to the lace where the Indians have broken through. Along vith the *Letters* of Cortés is the *True History of the Conquest of New Spain* by Bernal Díaz del Castillo, an ld soldier who spelt even worse than his contempor-ries, and began to write in a rage at a history pub-shed by someone else. In Bernal Díaz we have an ye-witnesses's account of what it was like to have een with Cortés, to have served under him and been ctually present on the most crucial occasions of the onquest of Mexico; while Cabeza de Vaca gave an ccount of the first attempt to settle Paraguay and the River Plate, and Alonso de Ercilla and Pedro de Oña omposed epic poems describing their experiences in he long wars against the Araucanian Indians in Chile. Mention must also be made of Bartolomé de las Casas, he "apostle of the Indies", whose passionate exposure f the exploitation and destruction of the Indians, in mines and plantations, was translated into many lan-uages and became the source of all the attacks made ubsequently against Spain and Spanish administration n America. It was Las Casas, unfortunately, who ecommended the importation of negro slaves.

One of the most attractive things about the writings f the conquistadores and early colonists is their vivid ppreciation of their new country. We can still admire he sense of fitness with which they set about the founda-on of new towns, and their striking success in planning reets, palaces and aqueducts. At the same time we are urprised by the power and freshness of their descrip-ons of Nature, and more especially in their feeling for

landscape. Modern travellers in Mexico are astonishe
at the truth and detailed observation in the narrative
written in the early years of the conquest; and readin
them at home gives almost as much pleasure as th
surprises and unexpected happenings of a journey t
Mexico, Chile, or Peru.

The life and manners of Spanish colonial society i
the large towns soon provided opportunities for satire
and satires on the inhabitants of Lima and Mexico wer
written at the beginning of the seventeenth century b
Rosas de Oquendo, a mysterious minor official, abou
whom not much is known. Dramatic performance
had been given in Mexico since 1538, though th
capital did not possess a permanent theatre until 159
This early date makes interesting comparison with th
dates of the first permanent theatre in London (1576–77
and Madrid (1579). A dramatist of real importanc
was Juan Ruiz de Alarcón, who was educated at th
University of Mexico before he went to Spain to con
tinue his studies at Salamanca. Though he returned t
Mexico at least once in the course of his life, most of h
work was done in Spain. He certainly influenced Cor
neille, and probably Molière as well, and is held to hav
created the comedy of manners. The last importar
Spanish American writer of the colonial period was Sc
Juana Inés de la Cruz (1651–85), an extremely learne
Mexican lady who lived in a convent because at tha
time a convent was the only place for a learned lad
to live. After the death of Calderón in 1681 she wa
indisputably the best poet writing in the Spanis
language, and her poems are still read to-day. Bu
imaginative literature in Spanish America never reall
had a chance in colonial times. The control of pape
and the vexatious regulations of the censorship mad
publication almost impossible; literature can hardl
exist in a society which lacks all freedom to express i
ideas. "The vassals of the King of Spain" (a vicero

nnounced in the eighteenth century) "should under-
tand once and for all that they were born to be silent
nd obey, and not to discuss and express opinions on
igh affairs of State." In judging this statement we
hould remember that even in England, in spite of
Milton's passionate plea for unlicensed printing, the
press-controller appointed by Charles II held that
'reading makes the multitude too familiar with the
ctions and counsels of their superiors".

In view of these insurmountable barriers, the need for
elf-expression led to an extraordinary development of
he plastic arts, which flourished not only in Mexico,
out also in Quito (in the modern republic of Ecuador),
Bogotá (Colombia), Lima and Cuzco (Peru), and
Potosí (Bolivia). The Mexican countryside is in many
listricts strewn with Baroque domes and towers, while
hardly a town in Spanish or Portuguese America is
without a group of noble buildings in the same style,
either in the great rectangular Plaza Mayor (big
quare), or in the straight streets intersecting one
another at right angles, and pointing, as often as not,
o a high mountain in the distance. Other legacies,
equally characteristic of Spanish colonial times, are the
great aqueducts striding across the bare landscape, with
nothing else in view except a strange, prickly cactus and
a distant volcano.

Spanish colonial art shows the plastic sense of the
Indian mason and wood-carver. The former not only
mastered an entirely new technique of building, but
brought something new into the Plateresque and
Baroque forms imported from Spain. Aboriginal influence is undeniable; designs and ornaments are to be
found taken from the flowers of the district, or from
Indian mythology. Façades are clothed with incredible
designs in coloured tiles; altars, ceilings, organs, pulpits,
choir-stalls, and confessionals are filled with intricate
wood-carving, and often covered with gold leaf which

glows still with miraculous beauty. This can be observe particularly at Quito in Ecuador no less than in Mexic and all the way from the original Potosí in Bolivia u to its namesake San Luis Potosí, 300 miles north Mexico city.

Potosí [1]—after Quito—is probably the best preserve Spanish colonial city in existence. It owes its founda tion, 14,000 feet up in the Andes, south of Lake Titicac to the mountain of silver and gold discovered in 153 which proved to be the nearest approach to Eldorad ever found by the Spaniards in America. The devalu tion of silver in the nineteenth century left the tow almost derelict, so that it stands to-day almost as stood four centuries ago, amid its Baroque architectu with strong Indian influences in the ornamentation.

The Portuguese in Brazil found no Indians with tradition of monumental building or any aptitude fo fantastic or imaginative decoration, like the original in habitants of Mexico, Guatemala or Peru. They had n portrait sculpture like the gentle archaic smiles of Toto nac terracottas or the caricatures of Peruvian pottery no woven fabrics like those of the pre-Spanish peoples the Valley of Mexico or the Andes. The first importan builders in Brazil were the Jesuits; but in 1637 th district of Pernambuco was captured by the Dutch, an what the earliest Brazilian architecture was like can b seen from the work of a Dutch painter, Frans Post, brought out by the new governor with a commission o scientists, to explore the jungle and make a record of th forests and sea-coasts. Post began in the characteristi style of Haarlem; but he fell for the exotic Brazilia scene, the tropical birds and flowers, and the startlin colours worn by the negroes, with the ludicrous con

[1] *Architectural Review*. No. 509, p. 165 (April 1939).

[2] See Robert C. Smith, in *Concerning Latin American Cultu* (New York: Columbia University Press, 1940). The work of othe Dutch painters in Brazil is described by T. Thomsen, *Albe Eckhout . . . und Moritz der Brasilianer* (Copenhagen, 1938).

ast of the staid efficient Dutch settler and his wife
earing the clothes they normally wore in Holland.
ltimately he developed a more theatrical and Italian
anner, with a practicable balcony, a palm-tree and a
opical flowering shrub disposed rather in the manner
an operatic stage set.

In the eighteenth century the emphasis shifts from
inting to architecture and sculpture. The Dutch had
een expelled from Pernambuco, and all the cities of
e Brazilian sea-coast were building monasteries and
urches. At Belem do Para, for instance, near the
ouths of the Amazon, the Jesuits built a severe renais-
nce cathedral which is still one of the largest buildings
Brazil. At Recife (the old Dutch capital) a church
as begun in 1749 to outdo the most spacious structures
Lisbon. At Bahia, which until 1763 was the seat of
e Portuguese viceroy, a whole succession of eighteenth
ntury styles may be seen; while the church of the
onceição da Praia (which was packed in numbered
ctions and brought over from the mother country)
ows what Portuguese building could be in its grand-
t manner. Rio de Janeiro begins a little later; the
eat square by the water-front, with the palace of the
ceroy, the cathedral, and the monumental fountain,
tes from the end of the eighteenth century.

But it was in the mining districts in the interior that
e greatest advances in Brazilian Baroque architecture
ere made. As at Potosí in Bolivia and Guanajuato in
exico, sumptuous churches, palaces, and convents
ose; and the buildings of the Brazilian mining dis-
icts (Minas Geraes) are superb in their convex façades
d oval towers. They also show Northern Portuguese
atures, such as a pilgrimage church at the top of a
mplicated spiral staircase (like the Bom Jesus at
aga) adorned with statues of major and minor pro-
ets, in the fantastic costumes and contorted attitudes
singers holding a long note during an operatic en-

semble. The architect in charge of this was a crippl
mulatto, nicknamed Aleijadinho, who achieved espec
distinction in his Baroque portals. The general desi
is one of "undulant pilasters, topped by fragmenta
Baroque arches carrying torch-bearing putti, wi
a medallion of involved sculpture representing t
Immaculate Conception".

In the nineteenth century the art of Brazil shared t
common fate of all Latin American art: romantic Eu
peanization. In the general admiration for Europe
culture, painters and sculptors from France and Ita
were invited to come over and take charge of architectu
decoration. In Mexico they did irreparable damage
some of the finest churches: the white and gold of wh
has been called the "Lourdes" style replaced many
the inimitable churrigueresque altars, and the carv
woodwork was either destroyed or allowed to rot
outhouses. Latin American art did not recover un
after the European war of 1914–18, with the murals
Diego Rivera.

Modern Literature

Spanish American literature came to life again in t
emotions aroused by the wars of independence. T
makers of Latin American democracy were inspired
memories of Voltaire, Rousseau, the Encyclopaedis
and the Revolution: it was useless for Spain—then
now—to claim spiritual hegemony over the Span
American peoples. They were now free, they said;
longer children of Spain, but of the victories th
had won over Spain. There remained their Span
blood and the Spanish language; but in three centur
the blood had become somewhat diluted, and t
language was no longer a bond except to the few w

ıvelled and the fewer still who read. "The Spanish nericans", it has been said, "had long ceased to form ;ingle people. Thrown back on themselves, occupied ly with their own affairs, they shut themselves in hind their frontiers."[1] The ocean, the Andes, the serts, and the great rivers were real frontiers; d though it was difficult to say where, for instance, gentina began and Bolivia ended, or where Peru ded and Ecuador began—even to-day it is difficult say exactly—yet these frontiers, however vague, were m the beginning Chinese walls for the peoples who d just gained their independence, and in a few years ese countries of the same language and much the me origin became separate nations which could not confused with their neighbours. They were as differ- t as Belgians and French, Flemish and Dutch, Swiss, ıstrians, and Germans. Each believed in its own premacy, in literature as in everything else, and erary rivalries were only avoided by their almost mplete ignorance of one another's writings. There ıs as yet no Latin American consciousness to cause e inhabitants of one country to take an interest in the lture of another. That was only brought about by rsecution, and the brutality of some of the dic- torships; and the country to profit most was Chile, ıich early in the nineteenth century became known a refuge for persecuted writers, teachers, and holars.

Bolívar's dream of a *patria grande* had not become a ality, even as a practical solution. The Spanish Ameri- n countries had been united for a few years during e war of independence, while they struggled for the me ideal against the same enemy. Bolívar had once ped to make them all into a single great empire; ıd some spirits in modern times (*e.g.*, Manuel Ugarte, ancisco García Calderón) have still dreamed of fusion

[1] Max Daireaux, *La Littérature hispano-américaine* (Paris, 1930).

on a large scale, to form a united front against the peaceful penetration of the United States.

Brazil stands definitely apart. It speaks and wri Portuguese, not Spanish, and Brazilian types and wa of living have provided a fruitful soil for the growth o genuinely national school of letters. Amazonia, d mond-hunters, negroes, the great desert plain of t Sertão, and miscellaneous folklore, have provided plen of subject-matter for modern Brazilian novelis Among them, José Lins do Rêgo is regarded as o of the leading prose-writers of contemporary La America.

A literary reputation in Latin America is not ea to win. The Nicaraguan Rubén Darío managed to ga his through the circumstances of his wandering li which obliged him to live in several different countr in Central and South America before he came Europe, and enabled him to publish in that great new paper, *La Nación* of Buenos Aires. Yet without tra abroad it was almost impossible for a writer to make name for himself, or a living. A Parnassian poet of gre distinction, Guillermo Valencia, is still (it is said) harc read outside Colombia, while the poet Amado Nervo the scholarly essayist Alfonso Reyes would never ha become so widely known outside Mexico if they had n been diplomats and lived in Europe and in Lat American countries other than their own. Until late (as we have seen) no reader in one Spanish Americ republic knew or cared what was being written another, unless he was a specialist or a careful stude of the literary supplement of *La Nación*. For the nar of a writer to become generally known in Lat America, it had to be known first in Paris and Madri and only the paralysis of Spanish culture by t Falange, and the occupation of Paris by the Nazis, ha driven Latin American writers to seek their fortunes and their sales—in their own countries. Buenos Air

d Mexico City—not Madrid or Barcelona—are now
: two most important centres for Spanish publishing.
Cattish critics used to remark that Latin America had
arge number of literary men, but no literature. That
10 longer true, if it ever was; there is to-day a vigor-
s, modern literature in Latin America, and it is the
pression of a genuinely American sensibility, a state
mind and way of looking at things which are common
writers all over the continent. That state of mind first
gan to show itself in the writers who were called
nodernist". The *modernista* movement was derived
rtly from the later French romantics, partly from the
rnassiens, while it developed later under the shadow
the *Symbolistes*. In France these schools had come one
er the other; in Latin America they arrived all at
ce. *Modernismo* became a desire to break away
m the literary forms and conventions which the
anish language had inherited from Spain and which
: Spanish romantic movement had reduced to mere
mbast and sentimentality. The movement was mainly
nong the poets, and affected all those who came after
: Colombian José Asunción Silva (1865–96). The
claration of independence, however, came from Rubén
río, with the book of poems called *Prosas profanas*
396). Darío was in fact the liberator of Spanish
etry and the Spanish spirit; since his time, no
anish poets in any part of the world have been able
resist him, though their poetic sensibility may have
oved into far distant regions since Rubén Darío died
1916.

A further result of the *modernista* movement was a
:urn to American subjects, notable in the later poems
Lugones (Argentina), Santos Chocano (Peru), and
errera y Reissig (Uruguay), as well as in Rubén Darío
mself (*Cantos de vida y esperanza*). This return to
nerican themes was encouraged by the work of a
narkable Uruguayan essayist, José Enrique Rodó,

whose chief books, *Ariel* and *Motivos de Proteo*, have b
been translated into English. The generation followi
him came under the influence of two shattering ever
which had a profound influence upon its internatio
outlook as well as on its aesthetic views. One was
Mexican revolution which began in 1910 but only ca
to a head in 1917; the other was the war of 1914–
with the revolution in Russia, and the dishearteni
developments in post-war Europe, leading eventua
to the outbreak of war in Spain in 1936 and its spre
to the rest of Europe in 1939. The effects on La
Americans are not hard to foresee. Men and wom
who have now reached middle age, as well as those
their thirties or even younger, all belong to a period
insecurity, typified, for some of them, in the rema
able revolt of university students against old-fashion
methods of teaching and administration, which beg
in the University of Córdoba (Argentina) in 1918, a
soon spread to other countries of Spanish Ameri
The net result of all these conditions is that La
American literature and art are both showing the eff
of that insecurity and sense of revolt, and, for the fi
time, are moving parallel to one another in a significan
modern direction. There is a violent objection to imi
tion, especially of things in Europe, combined with
deep concern for human values and for the rights of t
oppressed, whether they are Indians or whites, negro
or Jews.

Outstanding examples of this are the novels of Jo
quín Edwards Bello, in Chile, and several young
novelists in Ecuador, who have fearlessly attacked t
social problems of exploitation, unemployment, a
racial degeneration. The Mexican novelists have co
centrated on the seamy sides of the Mexican civil wa
Manuel Azuela in *Los de abajo*, Martín Luis Guzmán
El águila y la serpiente, and Rafael Muñoz in *Vamos c
Pancho Villa;* while Gregorio López y Fuentes, in

dio, represents another group of Mexican novelists ho draw their subject-matter from the modern Indian lage. *El Indio* may be compared with the novels of Traven, or with that striking novel of Mexico, by hames Williamson, *Sad Indian.*

Argentine novels are still haunted by the gaucho (see ge 54), though nothing has been written on that bject to touch the curious narrative poem—half epic d half autobiography—*Martín Fierro*, published in the venties of the last century by José Hernández. It has en described as the gaucho Bible, and certainly contins the whole of the gaucho philosophy of life, belongg to a time when the gaucho was to be seen at his best. here were not many consolations in that philosophy: usic, perhaps, and song, and above all the sense of ing a man on a horse, with the belief that all men ould be really equal if they could ride like a gaucho. he one man who understood this more than any other, d wrote about it in English, was the late Robert unninghame Graham, whose death, on the eve of the panish war, was an irreparable loss to British underanding of sides of the Spanish and Spanish American mperaments which are often misinterpreted. Another ucho epic, almost contemporary with *Martín Fierro*, *Fausto*, which relates—and relates with typically rdonic gaucho humour—the story of Faust as a ucho would have told it.

Sometimes the gaucho remains in the background, d makes his presence felt imperceptibly, without ever ctually appearing on the scene. Such is the case in e satirical short stories of life in a small town (*Pago hico*), and the novel cast in the form of the autoiography of a "politico": *Divertidas aventuras del nieto de uan Moreira*, by Roberto Payró. Yet without being nfair to the more recent Argentine and Uruguayan ovelists, Enrique Larreta and Carlos Reyles (who have lso taken the gaucho for their theme though they made their names through reconstructions of old Spain, à Maurice Barrès and Henri de Montherlant), it may be said that the only modern novel which can compare with *Martín Fierro* is *Don Segundo Sombra* by the late Ricardo Güiraldes (*d.* 1927). It is the story of a boy of fourteen, who runs away from his guardians—and only those who have been orphans left in the charge of unsympathetic guardians can realize what that means—to become a gaucho. The main motive, however, is not so much the gaucho life, or the escape from an unhappy home, but the personal devotion to the figure of Don Segundo, a horse-breaker and cattle-drover of the classical gaucho type. The curious thing is that the more the boy's admiration for Don Segundo increases the more real the boy becomes; while Don Segundo remains what he is, a shadow, *una sombra*, though always ready to help and encourage when his presence is needed. On two occasions he helps to raise his companion's spirits (like Sancho Panza) with typical stories in the manner of his people. But the boy, in spite of an unwavering determination to see the thing through, grows more and more discouraged as the years go by; and the unexpected news that his guardians are dead and that he has inherited an estancia and some money does not come a moment too soon. Modern economic conditions have made the gaucho a figure from the past; but it would be interesting to hear of some Argentine Cervantes, who, by describing the tragically comic adventures of a man who set out to revive the lost gaucho ideal in a world of petrol, barbed wire, and *frigoríficos*, should at the same time write the greatest of all gaucho romances. A certain solemnity in the temperament of most Argentine writers makes this improbable, and the peculiar requirements for Cervantesque humour seem more likely to arise in Chile. There the gaucho is as much a foreigner as he is in England, but a sense of humour seems be more at home than in some other parts of Latin merica.

Other outstanding modern novels (all of which have een translated into English) include *La Vorágine* by the olombian, José Eustasio Rivera. This concerns a urney, or rather an escape, into the Colombian lownd plains and jungle, with all the natural obstacles nd hardships of the tropics and many of the barbarities human oppression. It is made more poignant by the ct that the two chief characters, a man and a woman, ho undertook the journey for each other's sake, almost variably get on each other's nerves, so that the physil hardships are accompanied by corresponding mental nes. A modern novel of considerable distinction is *oña Bárbara,* by Rômulo Gallegos, a study of life nd the struggle against its injustice on the vast enezuelan plains sloping down to the Orinoco. It remarkable, among the majority of Latin American ovels, in that the chief character is a woman; while enezuela has also produced, in Teresa de la Parra, a riously Proustian woman writer, who takes as her bject women of her own generation; *Ifigenia* (1924) nd *Mama Blanca* (1928). An interesting work in autoographical form is the *Historia de una pasión argentina* by duardo Mallea, notable for the author's knowledge of nglish and obvious admiration for English literature, hich seems to have taken an important place in his evelopment. *Córdoba del recuerdo*, by Arturo Capdevila, a charming account of an Argentine childhood, passed ot among the gauchos but in an old-fashioned remote thedral town, before the arrival of modern progress.

Spanish American writers have sometimes comained that their own countries do not provide the nditions, the *ambiente*, favourable for writing. Others, e the late Enrique Gómez Carrillo, have even made ch embittered statements as that for a writer who had mething to tell the whole world (*pour un écrivain dont l'esprit est un tant soit peu universel*) the Spanish languag was in fact a prison. In England we have a somewh different opinion of the power, range, and beauty Spanish as one of the great world-languages of tl future; but Gómez Carrillo, like many Spanish Amer cans, had spent much of his life in Paris. He once told tl French critic Max Daireaux [1] that he would have give all his published work to have written one book French. This was not merely a piece of exquisite Spa ish courtesy; Rubén Darío had said much the san thing: "My dream was to write in French, and actually perpetrated some verse in that language The French studies of Rubén Darío bore fruit, in th they enabled him to increase the expressive and poetic qualities of Spanish.

Modern Painting

The tendencies which have appeared in the la twenty years in Latin American literature have al shown themselves in a remarkable way in paintin The immediate cause seems to have been the war 1914–18, for this brought many painters who had be living in Paris or Majorca back to their own countri in America. They returned to find it, in many wa virgin and unspoiled. They were also (they discovere artists with a universal reputation, and they were so given opportunities for showing what they could d Bernaldo de Quirós, for instance, was given the oppo tunity of producing a set of huge canvasses illustrati the life of the gaucho. Diego Rivera, back in Mexic found that his native land appealed to his imaginati as never before. Wall-space was offered him (as it w to Orozco and Siqueiros) for depicting the progress a ideals of the Mexican Revolution. The Indian far labourers, miners, soldiers, country schoolmasters, s

[1] *Op. cit.*, 32.

hemselves painted larger than life on the walls of im-
ortant government buildings, and endowed with a
lignity and importance they had never dreamed of pos-
essing. Other wall-paintings depicted great historical
vents, with the Indians in conflict with the Spaniards;
nd though the Indian was shown as the loser in the
var and the oppressed in the peace, the Spanish conqueror was more than once made to look ridiculous.
Other frescoes, again, showed popular Indian festivals
nd other aspects of genuine Mexican life. Their object
vas not only to decorate walls, but also to show the
Mexican people, numbers of whom could neither read
or write, what the history of their country had been
nd what its future might be.

The spirit which inspired the Mexican school of
ainting, as well as its technical methods, moved many
rtists in South America and the United States to follow
. The personality of Diego Rivera himself became
omething of a legend. "See that wall?" he said to an
nglish pupil, who had come with a view to taking
essons. "Well, go and paint it!" Those who worked
ith him or were influenced by him endeavoured to
evelop a style of their own in comformity with the
onditions of their own countries.

The light in Mexico is not the same as it is in Peru,
n the Argentine plains, the Bolivian plateau or the
haco. Cecilio Guzmán de Rojas, a Bolivian, did
ome sketches of the Chaco war which are as
oquent a commentary on war's futility as any ever
ritten. Meanwhile Candido Portinari had begun to
o for the Brazilian Negro what Diego Rivera had done
r the Mexican Indian. Up to this time the portrayal
the Negroes in Brazil had been a kind of sub-equa-
rial *Uncle Tom's Cabin*.[1] Portinari delineated the un-
ealized toil of the Negroes on a great coffee-plantation
his native state of S. Paulo as observed by himself.

[1] Robert C. Smith, in *Concerning Latin American Culture*, 194.

He also painted a number of very original portraits, an
then discovered a Brazil like that of Jorge Amado, th
novelist of Bahia, where "clowns play leapfrog an
Bahian women dance the carnival against the limitle
blue of the South Atlantic". Portinari, like Dieg
Rivera, Guzmán de Rojas, and Bernaldo de Quiró
have all shown in their different ways that Lati
American painting, "in spite of its exotic past an
constant borrowings from foreign sources, can be bot
monumental and original".

Modern Music

Painting and literature in Latin America flow alo
parallel channels, have their source in the sam
spiritual unrest, and aspire to the same ideal. I
their emphasis on qualities which are native to the sc
they may find the shortest path to real distinctio
In music, the same spirit is at work; there is a que
for a truly American musical idiom: "a new mus
for a New World".[1]

Before Europeans came, there was considerable d
velopment of music among the aborigines; and th
suggests the way to a new music which may be som
thing more than a mere continuation of Europe
tradition. How this pre-conquest music really sounde
or what value it may have to composers to-day,
only now beginning to be discovered;[2] but eviden
is obtainable from old instruments and from t
kind of music with which Indians in out-of-the-w
places still accompany their magic rites and ceremoni
and it proves to be music very different from th
of Europe, in rhythm and melody, and in the w
the scale is divided. Besides this indigenous Indi

[1] William Berrien, *ibid.*, 153.

[2] The *Boletín Latinoamericano de música*, edited by the Uruguay
Francisco Curt Lange, is indispensable for these questions.

ıusic, a Latin American composer can find new
hemes, new rhythmic patterns and harmonic structures
ı the music of colonial days and in the period of inde-
endence. This mestizo music is a composer's most
bvious source of inspiration; indeed, with its elements
erived from Indians and Negroes, Spaniards and
'ortuguese, music is probably the greatest cultural
ıstification for the race-mixtures in Latin America.

The Latin American composers of to-day are in fact
oing what Béla Bartók did in Hungary, Vaughan
Villiams in England, and Manuel de Falla in Spain;
ut they are doing it with the advantage of forty years'
ıusical experience—since Vaughan Williams first heard
n old man in Cambridgeshire singing "Bushes and
riars," and said to himself that that was the music
r him.

Popular forms of Latin American music are not con-
ned to the tangos and rumbas of to-day and their
ommercial imitations. A number of real popular
rms and rhythmic patterns have come into exist-
ıce in Brazil and Argentina; so that a Latin
merican composer of to-day has no lack of new and
citing material. "Real Latin American music," says
rofessor Berrien, "is something new and something
oung." The chief composers are Heitor Vila-Lobos
3razil), Carlos Chávez (Mexico), Juan Carlos Paz
Argentina), Domingo Santa Cruz (Chile), with Al-
nde, Roldán, García Caturla, Fabini, and many
hers. The composers of an earlier Latin American
neration wrote what was called *música universal*,
ough it was really only a pale reflection or dilution of
me European composer with an international reputa-
on. One might say that the difference between the
w Latin American music and the old is that between
aughan Williams and Elgar, Bartók and Dohnányi,
ılla and Turina—in a word, the difference between
ose who look forward and those who look back.

Neither Vila-Lobos nor Chávez are mere folklore com posers; neither is a nationalist in the narrow sense c the word; but each expresses musically what is in hir and has become part of him through his musical experi ence. Like Manuel de Falla, they seldom use a folkson or theme already existing in the music of their respectiv countries. They prefer to use their own original tune: but to present them in such a setting that they migh almost be taken for folk-tunes. Juan Carlos Pa prefers to employ an international idiom—the twelve tone scale; yet his music has a personal, individual qua ity, although to people who only listen with half an ea such music does not sound "typical". Like the nove of Güiraldes, Rivera, Azuela, Gallegos, and José Lir do Rêgo, like the painting of Diego Rivera, Orozco Siqueiros, Quirós, and Portinari, the best contempo ary Latin American music has a distinctly America flavour, and a decidedly American manner of sayin what it has to say.

Besides their own work in composition and conduc ing, improving the orchestras and the standard musical taste in the particular Latin American capit in which they may happen to live, most of the con posers mentioned are doing valuable work for music education. This is especially true of Vila-Lobos an Chávez. Vila-Lobos believes in the importance of mal ing good music of the past and present thorough familiar to children; his latest publications are a arrangements of classical and modern masterpieces f Brazilian children to sing. Chávez and Vila-Lobos a in fact but two more examples—two of the late examples—of that practical, clear-sighted America idealism, which, as the foregoing pages should ha shown, has never been absent from those parts America which were discovered and civilized by t Spanish and Portuguese.

CHAPTER V

PANAMERICANISM

THE word "panamericanism" first appeared in the *New York Evening Post*, March 5th, 1888.[1] The ideas it stood for were older, and went back to the time of Bolívar and Spanish American independence. Earlier still (1553) there was a remarkable petition to the Pope from Indian chiefs of many different races and languages in New Granada (Colombia), Peru and Mexico. Speaking in the name of all the Indians in the New World, they claimed equality with Europeans both as men and Christians and envisaged the union in the Holy See of all the American races.[2] Indeed, in spite of all the differences which have separated protestant-minded Anglo-Saxons from catholic-minded Spaniards and Portuguese and Indians, there has always been something to draw them together—a continental American point of view, shared by all the inhabitants of the new World. This point of view is the real starting point of panamericanism.

European writers to-day are apt to speak contemptuously of "Utopias". Sir Thomas More has been canonized—a wonderfully astute treatment for a communist—but the Saint's witty and subversive book remains unheeded. Americans, however, know from experience that an ideal republic can—with good will—be made a reality. North American examples are well known; South American instances have been referred to in an earlier chapter, and it should not be forgotten (though the fact is often obscured) that with the British colonists in the North and the Spanish colonists in the

[1] Eugène Pépin, *Le panaméricanisme* (Paris, 1938).
[2] M. Cuevas, *Miscellanea Fr. Ehrle*, III, 334. (Rome, 1924).

South there was always a religious motive, and that thi religious motive was perfectly genuine.

Panamericanism is the invention of visionaries anc idealists, the great object being the maintenance o peace on the continent of America. Its present signi- ficance is due to a quickening of the tempo at whicl old, idealistic themes are being adapted to moderr instruments of economic and political co-operation With the most important countries of Europe at war— nearly half the population of the world—the desirability of tightening economic bonds between the twenty-one American republics became increasingly evident, for the nations of the Western Hemisphere were being thrown more and more on their own resources. The European war gave panamericanism a new justifica- tion : the primary object was peace and the method "the permanent expansion of inter-American trade on a mutually profitable basis, in an atmosphere of political solidarity".[1]

The History of an Idea

The first step towards panamericanism was a meeting arranged by Bolívar in 1826 at Panama; it was attended by representatives from Peru, Colombia, Central America, and Mexico. The United States accepted, but one representative died on the way and the other arrived too late. The meeting supported Bolívar's proposals for the union of all the American countries, and a desire for closer communion be- tween the Spanish American republics dominated the next three conferences, called in 1847–48, 1856, 1864–65, to discuss intervention by the United States and France. These conferences showed, if nothing else, that the new republics considered them- selves a single family of nations.

[1] *Foreign Policy Reports* (New York, February 15th, 1940).

In one sense the panamerican movement was the idea 'James G. Blaine, Secretary of State under President arfield (1880). From the commercial point of view ere were sound reasons for encouraging closer business lations between the United States and Spanish merica. Many of its products could be admitted into e United States free of duty, without endangering the otective system then in force; while Spanish America uld absorb manufactures from the United States. he movement was to be "a diplomatic trade-mark" r the expansion of United States commerce; and r commerce the first essential was peace. At that oment, three of the Spanish American countries—hile, Peru, and Bolivia—were involved in a major nflict, and Blaine began by inviting the independent untries of America to a peace conference in Washing-n (1881). It was without effect. By requiring peace necessary for commerce, Blaine had put the cart fore the horse.

In 1889, however, all the independent governments Latin America (except Santo Domingo) sent dele-tes to Washington. The actual achievements were w, and did not come up to the plan originally pro-sed. The idea of a customs union, a *Zollverein*, which ould have been a great advantage to the United ates, was defeated; and an arbitration treaty, though ned by eleven nations, including the United States, led to be ratified. Yet this conference is regarded as he starting point of panamericanism as the tangible, ternational reality it is to-day"; and, most important all, the congress succeeded in creating an Inter-tional Bureau of the American Republics, which terwards became the Panamerican Union.

It is curious that neither at this congress nor at the ree which followed it (in 1902, 1906, and 1910) did y of the speakers mention the word panamericanism. ey referred instead to "American opinion", and

expressed the hope of the whole continent being able t
work together. The European War of 1914–18 made
difference. In the view of Secretary of State Lansin
panamericanism was the international policy of tl
Americas, as the Monroe Doctrine was the nation
policy of the United States; and since the fifth Inte
American Congress (Santiago de Chile, 1923) the wo
has been in frequent use.

Panamericanism in Practice

The Santiago Congress was not easy going for tl
delegates from the United States. Before their entry in
the war in 1917, and the appointment of Gener
Pershing to command the American Expeditiona
Force, that gallant officer had been across the Mexica
Border in command of a punitive expedition, playin
hide-and-seek with Pancho Villa. This act of interve
tion by the United States had not escaped the notice
Germany, and had led to a plan worthy of the ferti
brain of Dr Goebbels: the Zimmermann Note. Tl
German minister to Mexico was instructed to offer tl
Mexican Government an alliance with Germany, an
Mexico, after the German victory, would regain territo
lost to the United States in 1846–48, including Ca
fornia. The Zimmermann Note was intercepted by tl
British Intelligence Service, but it was a considerab
shock to the United States to learn that intervention
Latin America might come from Europe, and it becan
clear that one of the best ways of keeping forei
powers out of Latin America was to gain the confiden
of the Latin American nations themselves. Preside
Wilson endeavoured to line up the Latin Americ
republics against German imperialism. The line
formed was firm, but not complete. Eight republ
declared war against Germany, seven broke

plomatic relations, and four remained neutral: rgentina, Chile, Colombia, and Mexico. Mexico, in e frightful convulsions of a civil war, could hardly ave done otherwise. Brazil, on the other hand, suported the Allies wholeheartedly from the beginng; and it is only fair to add that, though the ficial attitude of Argentina was reserved, all the reublics of Latin America showed strong sympathy for e Allied cause, whether they remained neutral or ot.

When the war was over and the question of joining e League of Nations came up, the countries of Latin merica displayed the same independence of judgment ey had shown on the question of entering the war. In ite of the attitude of the United States towards the eague, important Latin American republics like rgentina, Brazil, Chile, Colombia, and Cuba joined . Some of them may have done so because they hoped that way to get help from other League members in ase the United States should try to intervene in their ffairs,[1] as it had in the affairs of the Dominican epublic, Haiti, Nicaragua, and, above all, Mexico. t any rate, the Santiago Congress of 1923 showed that ere had been a pronounced growth of Yankeehobia, and the fundamental divergence of opinion on e organization of peace-machinery left the congress ithout positive result.

Even the sixth congress, which took place at Havana 1928, still showed considerable antagonism to the Jnited States on the question of intervention; for in 926 the United States had landed marines once more Nicaragua. Though President Machado of Cuba poke of the constructive work of panamericanism—a opular will and a collective ideal leading towards niversal peace—the grievances of the Latin American

[1] Delia Goetz and Varian Fry, *The Good Neighbours* (New York, 939).

nations were not new. The panamerican movemen
they said, was really a Spanish idea, not an Anglo-Saxo
one. It had been born in the old Spanish colonies as
defensive reaction against interference from Europe
while the United States, which had seemed at first t
support the idea indirectly through the Monroe Doc
trine, had shown little practical interest, and ha
extended its territory to the West largely at the expens
of its nearest Spanish American neighbour, Mexic
After the Civil War, the United States appeared—in th
eyes of suspicious neighbours—to take the lead in
panamerican movement because it seemed to offe
every possible advantage for the development of Unite
States commerce. Panamericanism was a cloak fc
dollar-imperialism,[1] and neither Theodore Rooseve
with his big stick nor Coolidge with his dollar diplomac
can have been aware how deeply their action wa
resented in Latin America.

The "Good Neighbour"

Faith in international conferences had been shake
even by such purely American events as the Chaco wa
between Paraguay and Bolivia, the boundary disput
between Colombia and Peru, and the uncertain situa
tion regarding United States intervention in Cuba; whil
the failure of the world economic congress and the dis
armament negotiations at Geneva gave further caus
for despondency. But the Panamerican Conference a
Montevideo (1933) showed a fundamental and revolu
tionary change in the policy of the United States toward
Latin America. For the first time at a panamerica
congress, such controversial issues as debts were dis
cussed, and a resolution to lower tariff barriers wa
adopted unanimously. Most important of all was a

[1] E. Pépin, *loc. cit.*, 14.

;reement, also adopted unanimously, for the signature ıd ratification of all peace treaties. Finally Mr ordell Hull declared that "under the Roosevelt administration the United States Government was as much pposed as any other to interference with the freedom, ıe sovereignty, or other internal affairs or processes of ıe government of other nations".[1] While this was not definite renunciation of intervention, the position of ıe United States was made more explicit by President ranklin D. Roosevelt (December 28th, 1933) when he ıid that "the definite policy of the United States from ow on is one opposed to armed intervention". With resident Roosevelt, in fact, panamericanism seemed to ave dropped everything which could possibly be susect in the eyes of his Spanish American colleagues. He ad broken with all the old practices, and was trying to ıake panamericanism a real thing. He dedicated the Jnited States to the policy of the "Good Neighbour"—ıe neighbour who resolutely respects himself and, ecause he does so, respects the rights of others—ıe neighbour who respects his obligations and respects ıe sanctity of his agreements in and with world neighours. President Roosevelt showed that his acts were s good as his words. The differences with Haiti were ettled, United States troops withdrawn. The revolution ı Cuba (August 1933) would have justified recourse the Platt Amendment, which gave the United States ıe right to intervene to safeguard Cuban independnce or maintain a stable government. This time the latt Amendment was not invoked; only the naval ase at Guantánamo was retained. The Government f the United States refused to act in future as a debtollecting agency, or land marines in case of default n a loan. It also abandoned the policy of not recogızing revolutionary governments, including those in Central America.

[1] *Foreign Policy Reports*, February 15th, 1940.

In panamericanism, understood in its widest sen there are certain permanent ideas, far older than t word itself, aspirations which were there long befo the word was invented. The idea of solidarity, and t effective collaboration of all the American peoples go back (as we saw) to Bolívar, while its aspirations towar a firmly-based, permanent peace have never varie Gradually the theory of panamericanism had come include economic and political collaboration, and ideals had spread to all the democracies of the Americ continent. It had become "a vast movement of dem cratic, continental solidarity, tending towards a uni of all the American republics on a basis of perfect ju dical equality and complete independence with a vie to assuring peace on the American continent and pr moting among the American peoples relations of a kinds".

Moral Union

In December 1938 the Eighth Panamerican Congre met at Lima; and the idea of "moral union", which ha been developing ever since the last congress—mor union in defence of common interests—was able withstand the somewhat totalitarian scene staged Lima through foreign influence. Panamericanism, ali in its political and economic aspects, had made decided advance since the congress at Montevide the threat this time came from totalitarian penetratio into Latin American politics and economics. The were still doubts, in one or two quarters, of the disi terestedness and honesty of the United States. Son suspicion developed (through what agencies, it is eas to guess), that the United States was exploiting th fascist menace for its own interests. That menace wa the chief question at Lima, and it was noticed th while the United States delegates were obvious

vorried by the extent of Nazi and Fascist intrigues, the
Argentines regarded the matter with a surprising degree
of calm. The "Declaration of Lima" was a compromise
between these two opposing points of view, but it
exceeded all previous statements of inter-American
olidarity.

Its effectiveness was demonstrated at the meeting
of American Foreign Ministers on September 23rd,
939, just after the outbreak of the European war. The
'Declaration of Panama" established a wide "safety
belt", 300 miles deep, round the shores of the Western
Hemisphere. None of the belligerents recognized it;
nd the new policy met with a severe though incon-
lusive test on the occasion of the pursuit and scuttling
of the *Graf Spee* in the River Plate. At the Havana
Conference (July 1940), the second meeting of the
Foreign Ministers of the American republics, the chief
problem was hemisphere defence. The German in-
asion of Denmark, Norway, and the Low Countries,
he collapse of France, and the threatened *Blitzkrieg*
gainst Great Britain, had brought the war considerably
loser to the Americas, in a political sense as well as
n economic one. The Danish, Dutch, and French
possessions in the Western Hemisphere were no longer
ontrolled by friendly democracies, while the spread of
ostilities had had disastrous effects on the Latin
merican export markets.

To these grave events was added an alarming exten-
ion of Nazi and Fascist activities in Latin America.
They were aided in a subtle but scarcely less dangerous
nanner by the machinations of *Falange Exterior* (the
oreign branch of General Franco's organization in
pain), which, in collaboration with extremist elements
mong Spanish American clericals and sympathizers
vith Franco, propagandists, defeatists, and dupes, put
about that every true son of the Church must of
ecessity favour Franco, and therefore Mussolini, and

therefore also Hitler. The disappearance of Franc had caused some Latin Americans to lose intellectua interest in the war; the submission of Britain—a matte of small concern to the more ultramontane intellectual —seemed to be only a matter of weeks, and all that good Christian could do was to prepare himself, i humility, to accept the new order, from Germany.

The fall of France added to the fears that Germany if it should succeed in consolidating its power i Europe, would next seek economic and politica hegemony on the American continent. These fear were reflected in the pronouncement made on Jun 23rd, 1940, by the United States Minister to Uruguay "I am authorized (he said) to state that it is th intention and avowed policy of my Government t co-operate fully, whenever such co-operation is desired with all of the other American Governments in crushin all activities which arise from non-American source and which imperil our political and economic freedom.

At Havana, the outstanding achievement was th agreement reached on European possessions in th Western Hemisphere: no transference of such possessior to another European Power would be permitted by th American republics. Critics of this resolution complaine that it would once more legalize United States inter vention. But such intervention now could only b undertaken at the cost of undoing all that has bee done to make panamericanism a reality, and that is more lasting value to the United States than any increas of territory.

The Havana conference showed that panamericanisı was a living force. The American nations had deter mined to defend themselves against totalitarian pen tration of all sorts, and began by working out a metho for preventing any of the aggressor nations from takin possession of European colonies in the Western Hem sphere. The United States was authorized to take an

·mergency action which might be necessary to protect
hose colonies from seizure or attack.

The crisis through which Europe had been passing,
.nd the desire to keep out of it if possible, had done
nuch to develop a feeling for union in the Americas;
·ut the conviction that the New World could live its
·wn life, apart from the Old World, was disappearing.
:hen, just as it seemed that European intervention in
merica had come to an end, it reappeared under the
isguise of a new Hispanic "ideology", aimed at drawing
ome of the Latin American countries into political
ystems repugnant to American idealism.

Relations with Spain

Latin American relations with Spain had always
een important, and for the last forty years—ever since
ie Spanish American war of 1898—they had been
ordial. But when, in July 1940, the Spanish nationalists
roke off relations with Chile, they had such a bad
ress throughout Spanish America that they saw their
istake and resumed contact a few months later.
his incident, unimportant in itself, served to show
iat a question affecting the independence of action
any one of the Spanish American republics would
nite them against what had once been their mother
ountry. It was a diplomatic blunder on the part of
e *Caudillo*, which lost him and his régime much
mpathy in Latin America, and produced anti-Spanish
ntiments in those countries to an extent which had
ardly existed before. Many American Governments
ad been far from hostile to Franco, though the
iberal-democratic régimes of Mexico, Colombia, Costa
ica, and Chile had throughout been favourable to the
panish loyalists. The change to a cooler attitude
wards the rulers of Spain by the others was due to

several causes. There was first the unabated harsh-
ness of the new Spanish Government towards it
political opponents, and then the Nazi–Fascist activitie
in Latin America of *Falange Exterior*, referred t
before. Further, there were the pro-Hitler and pro
Mussolini attitude of the new Spain in the war agains
the British Commonwealth, and the diplomatic floun
dering of the Foreign Minister, Sr Serrano Suñer
Spanish American catholics were particularly offende
at his bad manners in going to Rome to see Mussolin
and not asking an audience of the Pope. Lastly, ther
was his misinterpretation of the word *hispanidad*.

Hispanidad formerly had a purely cultural signif
cance, and was a description of Spanish quality
Nationalist Spain had altered this to one which sme
strongly of Nazi–Fascist political domination; and, i
addition, had had the impertinence of attempting t
criticize the attitude of Latin American countries to
wards their own self-defence, exemplified in the matte
of the naval bases which were to be leased to th
United States. The new Spain had been guilty
other indiscretions, such as the officially inspire
articles in the Madrid press on "The Day of the Race
(*El día de la raza*), October 12th, the anniversary
Columbus's landing in America, and celebrated b
Spanish-speaking people all over the world. Lati
America was airily accused of "retarded development
which could be traced to the day when Spain lost he
"imperial vocation". Nothing could have been mo
irritating to Spanish Americans than this stupid stat
ment. It was as if Government spokesmen in Englan
were to declare that the United States suffered fro
retarded development traceable to the moment whe
Britain had to abandon her dominion there. *La Pren*
of Buenos Aires, an old, independent newspaper
conservative leanings, and one of the most influenti
organs of public opinion in the Spanish language, pu

lished a crushing reply which was widely quoted, and with approval, in other Spanish American countries. Officially, indeed, the Spanish Government had claimed no more than a "spiritual" axis in America. But the indiscretions of its supporters and the actions of its foreign friends had done much to direct the perennial Latin American suspicion of imperialist designs away from the United States towards another quarter.

ECONOMIC RELATIONS

Not less vital than the political relations between the American countries and Europe, and far more urgent from their immediate effects, are the economic relations between one American country and another.[1]

Some of the countries in both North and South America are organized to produce a surplus of certain raw materials for export. The loss of foreign markets for the usual export trade is bound to cause distress, and this has been all along the weak point in American economic defence. Some of the countries in the Western Hemisphere depend on their export trade to supply them with 70 or 80 per cent. of the goods which they cannot do without. The United States is more nearly self-sufficient; but it too has now serious disturbances in its prosperity, in the districts which have depended on exports now blocked by the war. The most difficult problems are found in a few strongly competitive products, such as wheat and cotton, which are exported from both North America and South; but it is hoped that the Export–Import Bank will enable fresh industry and trade to be promoted on terms which will give the borrowers a chance to succeed.

The international trade of the Americas was very

[1] *Economic Relations between the Americas* ("International Conciliation", No. 367, February 1941).

different in 1939 from what it had been in 1914. In both periods the United States provided the most important source of imports, and was the most important single market for the products of the countries to the south; but the United Kingdom and France were relatively less important in 1938–39 than they had been in 1913–14, while trade with Germany, though large and increasing, had not fully regained the importance it had before the first German war.

When the second German war broke out, interruption of South American trade with Europe was not at first so serious as it had been before; but the tightening of the blockade and unrestricted submarine warfare came more swiftly in 1939–40 than in 1914–18.

In Latin America the most noticeable effect of the present war was the rise in internal prices. Elimination of important overseas markets seriously reduced the purchasing power of countries which exported raw materials; and in view of the strict import control imposed by the United Kingdom and other members of the British Commonwealth, it seemed unlikely that South and Central American exports to these countries would increase, though they might change in character. South American exports of coffee and cotton were seriously limited, and the European market for corn and other foodstuffs was almost completely cut off. In spite of increased purchases from the United States, the internal buying power of the Latin American countries would have been seriously crippled if it had not been for the loans advanced to them by the United States.

Cultural Relations

"What useful contacts," some people have been asking themselves in the United States, "can be established in Spanish and Portuguese America, to ensure lasting peace?" What can be done without hurting the susceptibilities of so many different countries? For national vanities are like high-tension cable standards: it is dangerous to come too near them.[1]

In forming judgments on themselves, the Spanish and Portuguese American nations may be impelled by contradictory motives. Side by side with the increasing and not altogether disinterested praise from people abroad, there is a certain distrust—in some cases, excessive distrust—of their own countries. Yet we might expect new and beneficent forms of civilization in Spanish America and in Brazil, while Europe, stricken by the fatal errors of the past, turns its thoughts to this immense region where it is still possible to live in peace.

It is natural that the spirit of North America should expand towards the south, in much the same way as the spirit of England has acted on the South of Europe. There is a genuine good-neighbourly motive in all this—more than might appear at first glance to a wary Latin American; for people from the United States do really like to make themselves useful and help others, apart from the fact that at the same time they try to increase their markets. It is a very natural desire, and there is no hypocrisy about it, however strange and unaccountable such behaviour may be to people—in Europe even more than South America—who have been brought up on ruthless Latin logic.

Cultural intercourse between the United States and Spanish America and Brazil is now becoming more definite and more conscious, fortified as it is by official support. There are institutes, periodicals, and any number of special organizations, including a section of the State Department in Washington, entirely occupied with inter-American culture and friendly relations with the countries to the south. Some of the great

[1] Américo Castro, in *Agonía*, V. 93 (Buenos Aires, 1940).

Universities also are interested in the scheme, which is all part of the policy of the "Good Neighbour".

Conclusion

Panamericanism stands ultimately for what President Roosevelt has described as "the right to think, speak and act freely within the law and to have free access to the thoughts of others; the right of free association both national and international with one's fellow men; the right to live without fear of aggression, injustice or want; the right to believe and worship as conscience may dictate".

These rights are now threatened; Lord Halifax, in his first public pronouncement as British Ambassador to the United States, reminded his hearers that Nazi ambitions did not stop at Europe. Across what he called the "Straits of Dakar" the invader could swiftly pounce upon the Latin American good neighbours to the south. The American continent could be attacked before it had time to arm in self-defence; the doors of trade in Europe, Asia, and Africa would be closed to it, except on terms laid down by Germany.

"Self-interest," the United States Ambassador in London has said, "may hold nations together in temporary alliance, but common ideals are necessary to create the basis of lasting friendship between nations." Panamericanism is the creed of a Utopia, a dream of visionaries and idealists; but, like most other dreams in America, it has a firm practical basis and the support of that kind of practical idealism which has made American dreams come true. Through all its successive developments, the panamerican movement does not appear so much "a movement of collaboration imperiously demanded by the conditions of geography, race, production, and commerce", but rather the result of mutual give-and-take on the part of clear-sighted practical visionaries in Anglo-Saxon America in the north and Spanish and Portuguese America in the south. The ideas of these two sections, both national and international, were for long in opposition; it is only lately that agreement has been possible, in the face of common danger and the knowledge that certain non-American countries have used their influence to sponsor activities which, since they go dead against everything the American countries stand for, can accurately be described as "un-American".

In Europe, we have grown inclined to scoff at visionaries and prefer to listen to cranks. The lesson of the Americas—their importance and meaning for a distracted Europe—is that a Utopia, a New Atlantis, a City of the Sun, can not only be discovered but can be made to come true.

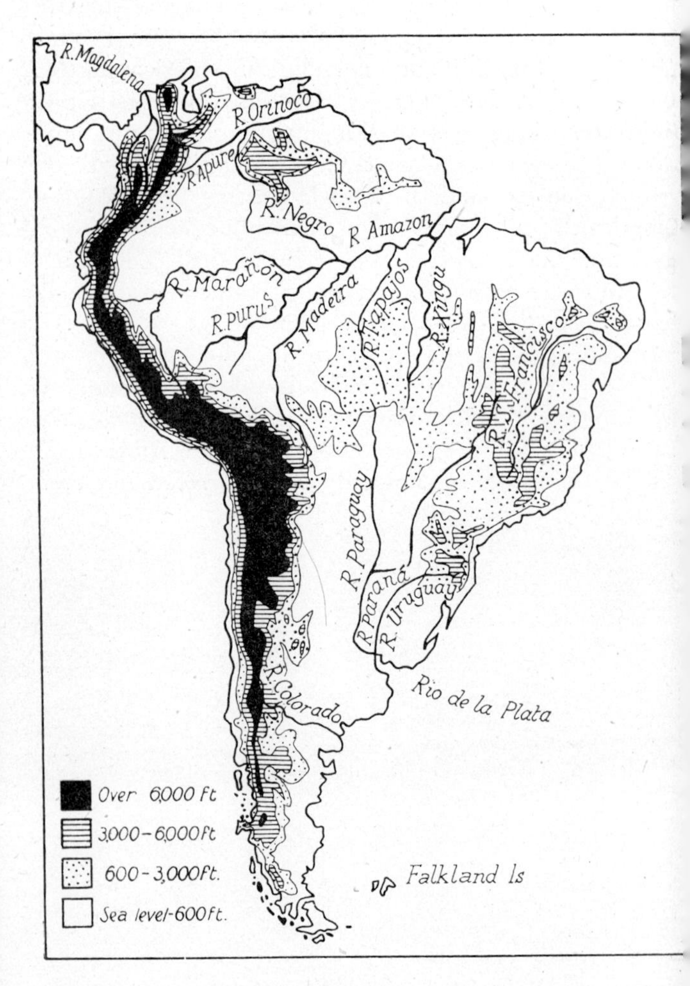

SOUTH AMERICA: PHYSICAL

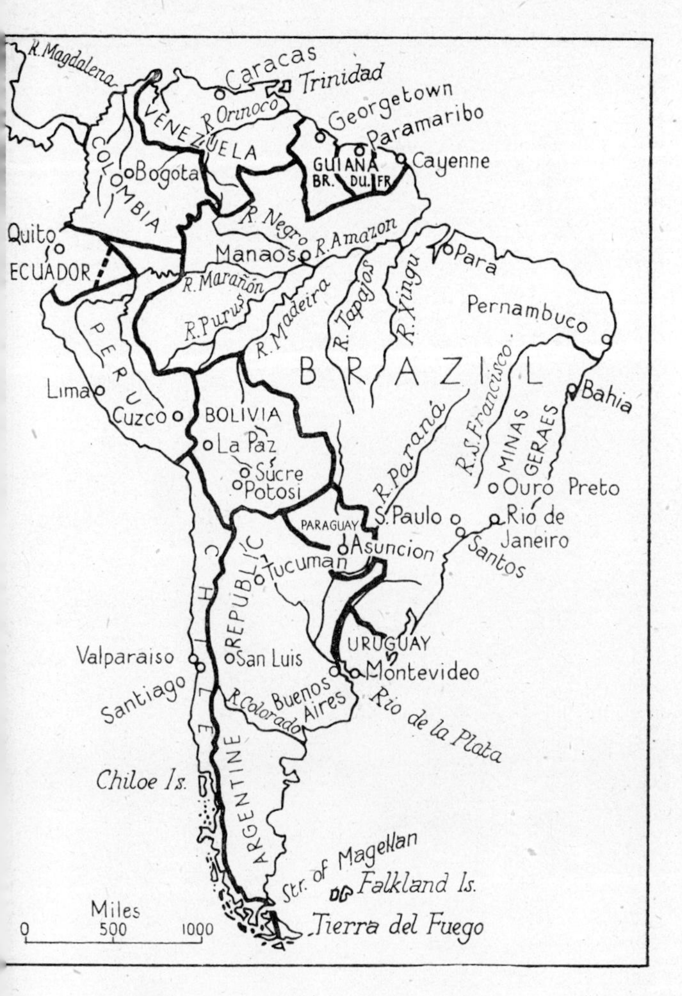

SOUTH AMERICA: POLITICAL

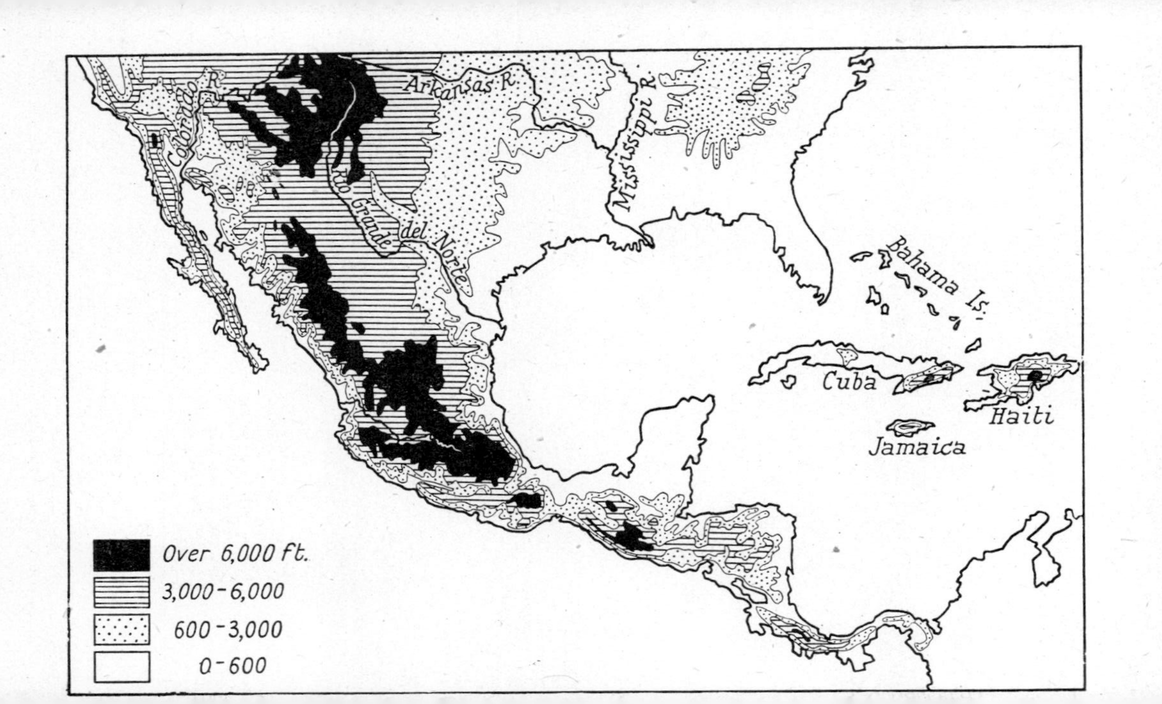
Arkansas R.
Mississippi R.
Colorado R.
Rio Grande del Norte
Bahama Is.
Cuba
Haiti
Jamaica
Over 6,000 ft.
3,000-6,000
600-3,000
0-600

MEXICO AND CENTRAL AMERICA: POLITICAL

BIBLIOGRAPHICAL NOTE

Besides the books referred to in the text, the followin
recent publications will be found useful:

Kirkpatrick, F. A.: *Latin America: A Brief Histor* Cambridge, 1938.

Humphreys, R. A.: *British Consular Reports on Lati America 1824–1826*. Royal Historical Society: Camde third series. Vol. LXIII. London, 1940.

Rippy, J. F.: *The Historical Evolution of Latin Americ* New York and Oxford, 1932.

The South American Handbook. London, 1941.

Kirkpatrick, F. A.: *A History of Argentina*. Cambridg 1931.

Levene, Ricardo: *A History of Argentina*. Translate and edited by W. S. Robertson. Chapel Hill, Nort Carolina, 1937.

Parkes, H. B.: *A History of Mexico*. New York an London, 1939.

Weyl, N. and S.: *The Reconquest of Mexico*. New York Oxford University Press, 1939.

Mackay, J. A.: *The Other Spanish Christ: a study in th spiritual history of Spain and South America*. Londo 1932.

INDEX

PRINTED IN GREAT BRITAIN BY RICHARD CLAY AND COMPANY, LTD.,
BUNGAY, SUFFOLK.